MAKE POSSIBILITIES HAPPEN

How to Transform Ideas into Reality

Grace Hawthorne
Design by Celia Leung

TEN SPEED PRESS
California | New York

HASSO PLATTNER
Institute of Design at Stanford

Contents

READY
SEE

START
DO

FINISH

A NO FROM D.SCHOO

At the Stanford d.school, design is a verb. It's an attitude to embody and a way to work. The core of that work is trying, to the best of one's abilities, to help things run more smoothly, delight more people, and ease more suffering. This holds true for you, too—whether design is your profession or simply a mindset you bring to life.

Founded in 2005 as a home for wayward thinkers, the d.school was a place where independent-minded people could gather, try out ideas, and make change. A lot has shifted in the decade or so since, but that original exuberant and resourceful attitude is as present today as it was then.

Our series of ten designer's guides is here to offer you the same inventiveness, insight, optimism, and perseverance that we champion at the d.school. Like a good tour guide, these handbooks will help you find your way through unknown territory and introduce you to some fundamental ideas that we hope will become cornerstones in your creative foundation.

Take a pause to gain a keen understanding of your everyday experiences in *Experiments in Reflection*. Look at the layers of oppression and uncover ways of working with others to create a more equitable world in *Design Social Change*.

Dive into this book to do just what the title says, *Make Possibilities Happen*!

love,
  the d.school

THIS BOOK IS A TOOLKIT TO SNAP YOU OUT OF ZOMBIE MODE SO YOU CAN SCHEME THE IMPOSSIBLE AND BRING YOUR PROJECTS, POTENTIAL, AND PROMISES TO LIFE.

THIS IS AN OPERATOR'S MANUAL FOR YOU AND YOUR

It is your personal guide to making sh*t happen—whatever that means for you—whether you are deep in the weeds or at square one. And we all know that, while it's really hard work, even little adjustments can completely change the velocity and trajectory of your work. This book is a blueprint for doing and mobilizing all of yourself; it will show you how working with the right tools, looking through new lenses, and cultivating a resourceful spirit will help you get it all done. Because without these things, you won't survive the difficult moments—and trust me, there will be many. Making things happen, even while in the midst of chaos, is possibility personified. Linking ideas to action is the miraculous process of transforming a thought into reality, reminding us that our work can design a better tomorrow not only for ourselves but for others too. Take your creativity seriously! Any work that you put out there *does* change the world in some way. Think of this book as a workshop open house, where the tools and processes are on full display for you to borrow and enlist in service of your creations and contributions to the world.

Creativity is at the crux of our humanity. It's enabled us, as human beings, to not only survive, but flourish!

Creativity is embodied in that awe-inspiring architectural wonder and in that exquisite bite of pasta, both of which stir us in indescribable ways. Creativity is intrinsic to that rocket launch or perfect sports play that make our hearts leap out of our chests and make our butts bound out of our chairs. Creativity fuels the innovation that helps educators teach children in the most difficult circumstances as well as the gadget that enables grandmas to connect with their families from afar. All creative outcomes—large or small, tangible or intangible—were all, once upon a time, just a possibility.

I have immersed myself in the study and practice of creativity and innovation over thirty years of making things and more than twelve years teaching design methodologies at Stanford's d.school, all the while shaping scientific research on creative capacity building and bringing new products to market. Through this work there is one thing I know for certain: we are all creative. We already possess (almost) everything we need to make things happen. Please know, I'm not an ordained high priestess of creativity bestowing upon you *the* secret book on possibilities from on high. We are all human, merely being. I am writing this book because I have dedicated my life to enabling and inspiring people to be creative, to helping others discover and release their inner genie-in-a-bottle through art-meets-commerce endeavors. A book that breaks down the nuances of how to materialize your own best ideas and efforts is another way to do just that.

THERE ARE MANY WAYS TO EXPLORE THIS BOOK.

PLEASE HACK IT TO YOUR NEEDS.

Possibility, in this book, is about the ability to see something in your imagination or in your heart and materialize it in real life. I've organized it to highlight the very simple actions that manifest the possibilities for our life, family, work, and dreams.

SEE

Visualize your desired outcome.

START

Just begin (this is everything).

DO

Show up and work.

FINISH

Follow through.

Sounds easy enough but the reality is these behaviors—see, start, do, and finish—do not come naturally to us; in fact, they are actually counterintuitive to how our human brain functions and our innate evolutionary dispositions. Our physiological tendencies, the constructs of our built environment, and our own emotions all get in the way. This happens often, with great frequency, and without us even knowing. This book will help you better understand how your brain is wired to think, so you'll be able to take charge and see your progress.

Within each section, concepts are organized into thought-sized chunks to ensure that you can fully absorb them in small spurts. In each chapter there are two sections: an opening section that engages the context of what and why and an activate section that ignites the content through THINKING and DOING. The doing section consists of adapted tried-and-true activities that I have used in my courses, workshops, and keynotes. Countless iterations of these assignments in Stanford University's classroom setting have confirmed that the brain can create new neural correlates (a.k.a. new and improved brain!) through the repetition of quick, time-constrained practice. All the activities for this book could not fit on these pages, so visit www.dschool.stanford.edu /possibilities-resources for the entire collection of activities, links, notes, resources, and more.

Ideally, to get the full value and maximum effect from this book, consume two chapters per week. It's not as much about the word count as it is about how you take in, process, reflect, and act upon the words on the page.

It's hard to begin, uncomfortable to not know, natural to question yourself, easy to be impatient, and challenging to swallow setbacks. Every single day we have an opportunity to positively alter our lives and other people's lives by making the inklings of our imagination real. And every single day we get waylaid by the routine minutiae of our daily tasks. But imagine if every little hunch or big harebrained idea that you conceived out of curiosity or in service of others came to life before your eyes. You don't have to imagine it because you are already standing in a reality of your own making; you just need to read or reread the updated operator's manual. This little book you hold in your hands right now explains the tools already at your disposal that can help you make possibilities happen. My hope is that this carefully crafted outpouring will enable and inspire you to feast at a buffet of possibility.

THIS IS IT: YOU ARE
ALREADY HERE.

ESTABLISH A POSSIBILITY, BACK IT WITH A CLEAR PURPOSE, MAKE IT BIG ENOUGH TO HOLD INTENSITY AND EMOTION, AND VISUALIZE IT AS CLEARLY AS IF IT ALREADY HAPPENED. THIS IS WHERE POSSIBILITY BEGINS.

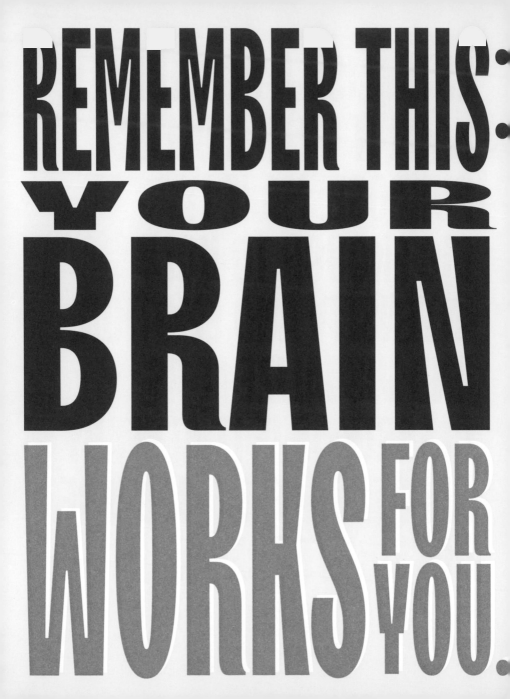

ESSENTIAL MIND TRICKS

ALTER YOUR MIND. Ten years ago, at the conclusion of Creative Gym—a d.school course I teach that focuses on developing the personal skill sets needed to foster innovation and creativity—a student named Dr. Daniel Hong, a brain surgeon visiting from Taiwan, approached me and asked "Am I different?" I told him, "Of course you are different; you just had ten weeks of creativity training!" He quickly shot back, "No, I mean, is *my brain* now different?"

This simple query of curiosity launched a decade-long research study focused on creative capacity building and collaboration at Stanford. Together with Dr. Allan Reiss and his Center for Interdisciplinary Brain Sciences Research at Stanford, Assistant Professor at Stanford Dr. Manish Saggar, the Hasso Plattner Institute at Potsdam, and the Stanford d.school, we embarked on a journey to define creativity and its underpinnings in an innovation context. We wanted to know whether we are born with a fixed level of creativity or if creativity is acquired knowledge, like riding a bicycle. And if we could we teach people to become more creative through conditioning the mind as we would a muscle. This research led to groundbreaking work, which found that creativity is a state of mind that can be taught and conditioned. After undergoing the creativity training from the d.school's Creative Gym course, not only was a subject's brain rewired, but they produced more highly rated outcomes on creative tasks.

This was significant for scientific reasons. It was one of the first crossover longitudinal studies on creativity of its kind, and the results were not the typical self-reported assessments frequently used in difficult-to-measure situations. Instead, the combination of fMRI brain scans and a battery of neuropsychological tests administered to the participants indicated that there were physiological changes in the brain as a result of this creativity training. As educators dedicated to transforming students, we always wonder how effective our work is, so we look to the anecdotal evidence of our students' real-world achievements as a barometer. But that kind of self-efficacy can't match the evidence from fMRI scans, which visibly show us that the participants' brains are different. These scans reveal that the brain responds to and evolves with creativity practice and conditioning over a relatively short period of training. You *can* alter your mind, both literally and figuratively by training your brain to innovate and create. (For even more ideas on how to do this, check out *Creative Acts for Curious People* by Sarah Stein Greenberg.)

DROP THE PALEOLITHIC TENDENCIES. Some of our brain's wiring is inherited from our hunter-gatherer Stone Age ancestors, who lived nearly 200,000 years ago. To survive back then, the human brain was biased toward comfort, certainty, and safety. Flash forward to today: our brains still have that bias. Making possibilities happen goes against those enduring primal tendencies because it's risky and uncertain. Back then, safety equated to survival, but today those same behaviors may lead to stagnation. From our evolved intellectual viewpoint, this safety bias is sometimes described as being "a little soft in the belly," but it is a natural tendency developed millennia ago.

So how can we sidestep our brain's risk wiring without throwing out the physical safety bit in its entirety? If the cave bear of our ancestors is the disinformation metaverse for us today, let's deploy a "mind dodge," a simple mind trick that uses the power of consciousness to guide our thoughts rather than letting them guide us. When we are aware of our unconscious tendencies and also know that we can change the wiring that doesn't serve us, we can dodge our minds' inherited predispositions. Here are three essential mind dodges to do just that.

KNOW YOUR BIAS TO WHAT YOU ALREADY KNOW. Your brain is a repository of all your prior experience— it's mapped with all your cumulative emotional, cognitive, and motor experience to at least age twenty-five. That alone restricts your ability to think without limits. Your memories define how you perceive, process, and act without your knowing it. This is how we make sense of things. We are typically uncomfortable in unfamiliar situations that don't make sense—they are disorienting and disturbing and disrupt the brain's sacred trinity of comfort, certainty, and safety. But being tied down to the familiar keeps you from seeing possibilities. Don't let your default (your unconscious biases) hold you back. Intentionally act outside of the familiar by not always sticking to your usual (drink choice, route home, schedule, and so on) and explore the full potential of your life.

USE YOUR THOUGHTS AS FUEL. When Rolf Landauer, a German-American physicist and a forerunner in the field of quantum computing, famously declared in 1991 that "information is physical," it set off studies aiming to test the theory that information is a fundamental component of the physical world. Landauer postulated a theory that information is physical and thoughts are energy— a theory deeply debated in scientific circles. If we think of our thoughts as conducting energy in the same way data can be transmitted as electromagnetic waves to our phones and computers, it's not far-fetched to make the next imaginative leap:

WHERE THOUGHTS GO, ENERGY FLOWS.

Thoughts carry a vibrational frequency in the form of energy. Albert Einstein sums it up with "everything in life is vibration." I like to imagine thoughts are akin to a tuning fork, resonating with other similar tones. I notice that my positive thoughts tend to call on and resonate with other positive thoughts. A visible manifestation of this concept can be seen in the audible resonance of cello or piano strings: when two notes are one octave apart, one has a frequency exactly two times higher than the other, and even though that note has twice as many waves, the two notes reverberate together and sound like one complete note. When playing one note and looking at the strings, you can visibly see (and hear) the other one vibrate in resonance.

If thoughts produce energy that can recruit more like energy, we should all be using our thoughts resourcefully by enlisting them to serve our possibilities. This comes in handy when you face a huge task that feels overwhelming. Negatively dreading the huge task will only generate procrastination and lethargy, while positively accepting the task will set up a chain reaction of initiative and action, much like the resonating neighborly notes of a stringed instrument.

PAY ATTENTION TO YOUR ATTENTION. Be the badass bouncer at the entrance of your mind. Carefully choose which thoughts you allow through. This means you have to be incredibly attentive to your attention. It's easy to notice negative news, to dwell on fears or unproductive emotions like worry, regret, should have/could have. Psychologically, humans have a natural negativity bias. Studies show that people tend to pay more attention to negative stimuli than positive ones, give more weight to negative pieces of information over positive ones when making a decision, and assign stronger emotions to negative events versus positive ones. Case in point: when you chat with a good friend, do they bend your ear with all the great things about their partner or do they tend to complain about their partner's shortcomings? If negativity tends to be our default mode, be mindful about where you place your attention and place it only on what you want, not what you don't want.

THINKING. Taking command of your thoughts is the core concept required to efficiently direct your energy toward your desired outcome. Knowing our tendencies allows us to act in a deliberate manner in the service of our possibilities. Knowing that the human brain is wired to seek safety allows us to make decisions outside of that comfort zone. Putting yourself in a place of potential discomfort takes some willful practice. Yes, it may be difficult the first few times, but with practice you can learn to embrace the discomfort and benefit from it.

REDIRECT YOUR THOUGHTS AND EMOTIONS AROUND UNCERTAINTY
TO REVEAL NEW POSSIBILITIES.

DOING: DO A DUCHAMP. Marcel Duchamp was one of the most influential artists of the twentieth century. He famously took a discarded ceramic urinal, turned it upside down, and called it art. It threw the art world into an uproar. How can you call that art?! Ariel, in the animated film *Little Mermaid*, picked up a fork from a sunken ship and used it as a hair comb. Both of these examples are a variation of an activity we run at the d.school. It is also inspired by the Alternative Uses Test, a popular psychology assessment tool designed by J.P. Guilford in 1967 that evaluates divergent thinking abilities—basically, how flexible and creative the person can be. The intention is to bypass preconceived notions of an object's purpose. A fork is no longer just an eating utensil; it can be a hair comb, a garden sign holder, a marshmallow roaster, a mini loom, a cake decorator, a back scratcher, and so on. Once you master this ability, an entirely new set of possibilities opens up. Letting go of what you already know allows you to see and conceive of an explosion of new ideas. This activity will help increase the flow of your creative juices from a trickle to a tempestuous gush.

Reach for an everyday object on your desk. Set a timer for 60 seconds.

**On a piece of paper, jot down
other uses that object could have
that aren't the known or intended
purpose. Go as quickly as you can.
Go for quantity.**

> *Stapler:* garlic smasher,
> photo easel, shoe heel . . .

**Repeat daily with two objects,
two times per week, for a month
and see how you progress.
It may not take very long for this
ability to become second nature.**

After your first effort, count the number of other uses
you wrote down. Make a note of your level of ease.
Did you have a difficult time coming up with ideas, or did
your pen have a hard time keeping up with your brain?
How did it feel differently the fifth time you did this?
If you save your iterations of your output over time, you
can reflect on your progress. This is a great go-to activity
when you are feeling stuck. We run this activity during
class in teams as a competition with a box of limited
objects and rapidly changing themes. You'd be amazed at
what a simple spatula can become in different contexts
such as a shopping mall, restaurant, circus, and more.

IMAGINE YOUR IDEAL OUTCOME, AND FLESH IT OUT IN EXCRUCIATING DETAIL.

BUILD YOUR OWN MATRIX

ENVISION WITH INTENTION. If your mind cannot conceive of and believe in your possibility, you won't be able to achieve it. Envisioning your possibility as a fait accompli, bathed in rich detail, brings your project that much closer to completion. Knowing this, one way to bring your possibilities to life is to build your own matrix—the environment in which you are building your life. Begin by defining the context from which your project will be created. To build your matrix, think about your project with these three vectors: purpose, vision, and goal.

HAVE PURPOSE. Why is your project important? What is the intention behind it? Having a purpose is the departure point to all possibilities and achievements. Moving toward an accomplishment that is meaningful to you gives you the energy to get through it. It can be whatever you want it to be; you have absolute control and power in determining your purpose or possibility. Instill your purpose into both the macro of your life's work and the micro of an individual task. Purpose points to our existence at the most fundamental level of being. With a definite purpose, you can create a clear picture of what you want.

HAVE VISION. How will your project interact with the world? What will make it better? Your vision is a mental image of what has not happened yet. Use your imagination to see what does not yet exist. If you conjure an image clearly, with rich detail, you should be able to feel like you are there. Having a vision does not guarantee it will happen, but not having a vision guarantees it won't. With a vision so clear, bold, forward thinking, and purposeful, conviction shows up and leads the way. Remember that visions come from the heart; goals and objectives come from the head. Your vision is not the realization of the goal; it's everything else around it, namely the emotions you will experience, the people who will be positively impacted, and what it will feel and look like in that moment.

HAVE A GOAL. What do you hope to accomplish with your project? What will attaining your goal mean? Goal setting is usually very challenging for people because it's hard to right-size a possible project to the dimensions of time, scale, achievability, and importance. Sometimes people have too many goals and can't focus or are unsure how to prioritize them. Setting milestones to help measure progress is helpful in keeping efforts focused. If you don't have a goal, you have nothing to shoot for, and you are leaving things up to chance. Just having one is essential to achieving it.

SEE WHAT YOU ARE NOT SEEING. What you see through your vision is not just the images physiologically captured by your retina. Retinas serve up so much visual information that the brain can't take it all in. Instead, the brain makes it manageable by picking out the bits it recognizes and fills in the rest with what it already knows. Yes, everything you "see" is continuously being shaped by your personal context, essentially all that you know. It is impossible to look at the world and our lives without seeing everything through a moving kaleidoscope of memories, disposition, past experiences, heritage, and so on—all the things that shape our identity. I frequently share in class a famous quote that perfectly expresses this idea:

"WE DON'T SEE THINGS AS THEY ARE, WE SEE THEM AS WE ARE."

I've been attributing this quote to the author Anaïs Nin for more than a decade now. Upon further investigation, I found that it actually has a long lineage of usage and origin, dating back to the 1800s. Regardless of its source, I love this quote because it leaves you holding the bag. It inspires you to take responsibility in a dimension that no one ever gets to see—your mind. It also succinctly sums up the power of perception—the intersection between what your eyes see and what your brain perceives.

CHOOSE YOUR PERSPECTIVE. You have the freedom to choose what you perceive. Because we cannot disconnect our memories from what we see, we have a tendency to amplify and focus on the things that we *want* to see based on past experience. When we become aware of this, we can see more intentionally by choosing how and what we see. This informed ability is what we'll call our *purple lens*, because actual violet lenses provide enhanced color and contour perception. Proverbial purple lenses are a tool at your disposal now, where you can consciously make a deliberate choice about how to perceive a decision, event, person, and so on.

If life is part genetics, part circumstance, and part perception, only one of those is really under your influence— and that is perception. Lean into it. Choose what you see and how to perceive it. As with any other skill you seek to master, you can get really good at shifting your perspective with practice and awareness, regardless of how you may feel emotionally. In our class, we practice toggling dimensions with some basic optical illusions like the Necker cube, a two-dimensional representation of a three-dimensional wire frame cube. Students learn to flip back and forth between alternating perspectives of the same figure. While it feels awkward and foreign at first, it quickly becomes a familiar tool in perspective.

THINKING. A purpose can be a small tremor or a towering tsunami. It can be as fleeting as a whisper or it can be huge, nagging, and persistent. These rumblings of purpose are points of synthesis that your mind is giving you in the form of a gift. These gifts are your intuition talking, so don't ignore them. Instead, capture them in a journal, sticky note, scrap of paper, your phone, wherever. They can be complete thoughts in and of themselves or pieces of a larger puzzle you're still putting together. Inklings, large or small, are just the tip of the iceberg. Crystallize them. The more clarity you have, the easier it will be to persist through the hard work of manifesting ideas in the real world.

SEE THE OUTCOME YOU DESIRE WITH CLEAR PURPOSE AND VISION TO MOBILIZE YOUR MOTIVATION.

DOING: CRYSTAL CLEAR. Visualization is a great activity that allows you to envision what could come to be. Elite athletes do this all the time. They visualize the outcome they want to achieve before they compete. These mental images of a positive future outcome prime our subconscious emotional state and promote calm and confidence. Additionally, these mental images get stored in the mind as something akin to a real memory. Our minds can't tell the difference between something vividly imagined and a real memory. What's efficient about this is that our subconscious brain continues to work on the visualization without being aware of it. Consider it a mental rehearsal. You see and feel the situation and the outcome you desire so clearly in your mind that your brain creates a muscle memory of that possibility. The following activity will help kick-start your habit of visualization.

Write down one of your goals— a recurring item that you've thought about doing but for one reason or another haven't taken the first step.

Now close your eyes for a few minutes and see yourself completing and/or achieving these things. See all the glorious details of what that looks like: where you are, who is there, what you are wearing, how you are feeling. Vividly see yourself celebrating and witnessing the success of the event.

Now imagine yourself after this celebration of accomplishment. You've done it! How does it feel? Jot down your emotions.

Visualize right before you fall asleep! If you visualize with regularity right before bedtime, you're essentially providing work instructions for your subconscious for at least a few hours after you fall asleep.

Combine this tool of visualizing what you want to happen with paying attention to your attention, and you'll have the one-two punch to help set the mind's stage to that desired end. This is somewhat analogous to the theory of target fixation, a behavior in driving whereby the driver tends to drive straight into the singular object they are focused on. The simple fix is to not look where you don't want to go! Similarly with visualization, set your worries aside and create mental images of only what you want to happen.

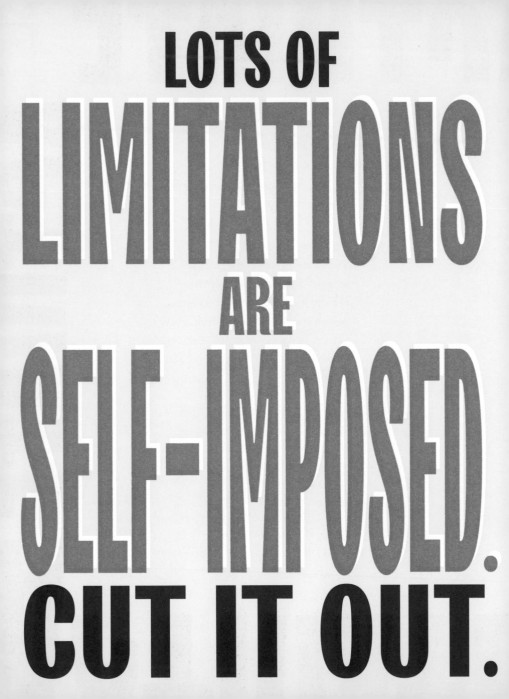

LOTS OF LIMITATIONS ARE SELF-IMPOSED. CUT IT OUT.

ILLUSORY
BOUNDARIES

BE BOUNDLESS. Boundaries are imaginary lines that separate two things. The operative word here is *imaginary*. Most commonly used to demarcate property or country lines geographically, a boundary is also defined as something that signifies a limit or an extent. Most boundary lines are not physical, iron-clad walls that separate. Two types of boundaries are germane to the topic of possibilities, namely internal and external.

INTERNAL BOUNDARIES. We often set personal boundaries to compartmentalize space, ideas, or groups where we want to keep a distance. Living within our boundaries is a place we feel comfortable—*I'll be okay here.* While some internal boundaries are essential for maintaining our mental health, other internal boundaries are emotional constructs of our own making. Knowing the distinction between what's healthy versus what's constricting will help crack open possibilities. Constricting, self-imposed limitations are usually the old stories we use to reinforce our existing behaviors. These personal boundaries are often constructed from the self-limiting beliefs we create to protect ourselves—things like *I don't have time*, *I don't have X resource*, *I don't have that* *connection*, [fill in the blank]. Dr. Bernie Roth, a legend in the Stanford design scene and one of the cofounders of the d.school, will be the first to tell you that excuses like these are bullsh*t. Throughout our lives, our internal monologue is our primordial brain seeking to reduce risk. Once we examine our internal objections to a course of action, we often find that our "objections" are merely self-imposed boundaries.

Not all personal boundaries are self-limiting. The healthy ones are downright mandatory. The key is knowing which ones are holding you back. Ironically, the opposite is also true. Thinking you know everything already is also self-limiting. "I know" can create a kind of blind spot because it's a barrier to seeking or seeing another option. Either way, being aware of your self-imposed internal boundaries and blind spots takes intentional, applied awareness.

EXTERNAL BOUNDARIES. Some external boundaries are used to create collaboration and flow; others are installed to exclude and control. Some external boundaries are more bendable than others. Society is built such that different people have varying amounts of agency to change boundaries. Also, some external boundaries are more useful to adhere to than others. Traffic signals are a great example of an external boundary that is rigid and aims to create safe roadways for all. It makes sense to respect these boundaries. However, everyday life has other, more flexible boundaries, including the limitations on how we think the world works. Thoughts like *Unless I get X, I won't* *be able to achieve Y* are debilitating because we are letting self-imposed external boundaries restrict what is truly possible. Not every situation is ever so black and white if you stop to examine it more closely.

Could boundaries be a method for our mind to create certainty where none exists? Nothing is ever truly guaranteed, and the truth is often a matter of perspective. Even in math and science the truth can vary by perspective. Statisticians and accountants know this de facto; while data is perceived to be numerically calculable facts, how you interpret the data can vary. I am reminded of my first job out of college as a CPA for a large accounting firm. From afar, it seems like accounting represents a binary, numerical truth. However, even accounting reports can be open to interpretations, in the same way the final score of a football game doesn't always reflect how hard fought the game really was. Another example is the word *no*. I remember a lecture by the head of a large Hollywood agency telling a group of grad students that rejection is not personal or absolute, it's just a data point. Know that *no* is actually *not right now*—it is never the end if you can help others see new possibilities.

Fundamentally, not questioning perceived boundaries can keep you from possibility. Once you acknowledge that some boundaries are more flexible than they seem, they will dissipate and new possibilities will appear in their place. Instead of trying to pad a potential fall with self-limiting thoughts that curb your best ideas before they have a chance to emerge, be a champion of hope and take a risk.

RECOGNIZE YOUR WORTH. When companies get acquired by other companies, there are industry formulas and metrics that determine the value of the business. The type of business determines the valuation parameters. Depending on the type of business, there are different characteristics that determine value; for example, revenue or the number of subscribers. One method of determining a company's value is by looking at its future potential value, not its past. In finance this is called the "present value." The present value of a company represents the current value of its future potential earnings—that is, the value that business can generate in the future. A company that is not earning any money today but is expected to earn millions of dollars in the future will have a valuation based on that bright future. This is important because the concept of value also applies to you. Your current value is based on your future potential. A common self-imposed boundary is time—although we value companies based on what we think they can accomplish in the future, we value ourselves based on what we have already accomplished. What you could someday do in this world is your potential. Guess what? You are likely undervaluing yourself by not factoring in your future potential.

THINKING. Going beyond boundaries does not mean surrendering your fate to outcomes you can't predict or control. Leap past the *why* or *why not* and dive all the way into the *how*. While you may not be able to control the outcome, you can control your effort and self-imposed limitations. Have faith that you will do what you can do and you will handle what comes. Being unbound is part of trusting that you can be resilient no matter the outcome. You can go as far as you're willing to let yourself go.

DON'T WONDER IF YOU CAN; KNOW YOU CAN DO WHAT IT TAKES TO GET THERE.

DOING: SERENITY SORTING. As mentioned, some boundaries are real and hard to overcome; others are imagined and, with the right perspective, turn out to be quite flexible. The key is being able to understand the elements in a situation that you can control versus the ones you cannot control. This understanding is essential to peace of mind, because you gain more freedom to focus on the things you do have control over if you can disassociate yourself from things you cannot control. Once outcomes are sorted this way, you no longer have to expend useless energy. Examples of things you cannot control: Will you get the job? Will that person love you back? Will it rain tomorrow? Is there a global pandemic? The Serenity Prayer, first documented in the eighth century, calls for accepting the things you can't change, changing the things you can, and being wise enough to know the difference. Merely reading the quote and contemplating it is a good starting point, but insufficient for making possibilities happen. Here's an activity that'll give you a framework to write down the stuff that hinders you and then determine systematically whether it is something within your control or not. This process is quite liberating!

Write down three things specific to your project that you have concern, worry, or wonder about.

Next to each item, note whether it is in your control or not. If you need to extrapolate the item into a few components and then make the determination, feel free.

> **Wonder:** *Will the deal go through?*
> **Extrapolated:** *deal terms, company directives, world economic health, board outlook*

If it's within your control, write down a couple of things you can do to affect it. If it's not within your control, let it go and reallocate your energy where it can make a difference.

World economic outlook is out of your control, but shaping deal terms so the deal has maximum impact in a particular economic climate is within your control.

We created this activity for a d.school course titled Fail Faster. The premise is that failure is a necessary precursor to success. When failure happens often and early and when the stakes aren't so large, you allow yourself more time to make the adjustments that help you get to a better outcome more quickly. This also transforms the concept of failure from a negative perception to an essential one. Acknowledging what you cannot control is a fantastic filter that allows you to allocate your efforts and energies more productively.

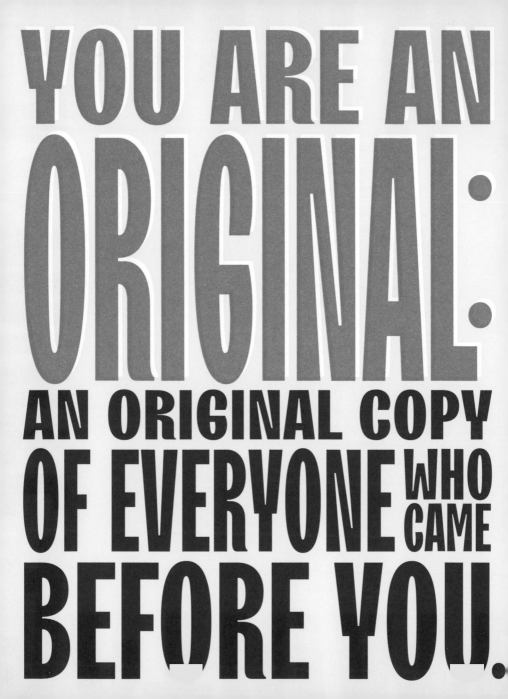

YOU ARE AN ORIGINAL: AN ORIGINAL COPY OF EVERYONE WHO CAME BEFORE YOU.

SYNTHESIS AND ORIGINALITY

BE(ING) ONE OF A KIND. Lots of theories purport that there is nothing new in this world, anywhere! Not in music or fashion or literature or art or anything else. In essence, this means that every idea is just a remix of one or more ideas that came before it. This truth is inescapable because you cannot divorce yourself from what you know. And what you know is what you've seen. Most of the time, we are indeed piecing together ideas that came before us.

If we roll forward under the assumption that there is nothing new, we need to consider how we talk about new ideas. When we embarked on our research study on creativity, our team spent an enormous amount of time defining what "creativity" meant. For the project, we defined creativity as "a state of being" and the ability "to synthesize novel connections and express meaningful outcomes." Note that this statement focuses on making new connections, not creating new ideas from scratch.

We all build on the ideas that came before us, but the ideas you express are unique to *your* experiences, and how you express them is a product of *your* unique skills. Even the way you process the intake of any idea is wholly yours.

Two different people, same input, two different interpretations. Take a note from filmmaker Jim Jarmusch: "Nothing is original. . . . Authenticity is invaluable; originality is non-existent." Do not underestimate the value of your own experience. All the things that only you notice because they strike you (for whatever reason) are what make you *you*. Originality is not the point—your one-of-a-kind, honest take is what matters.

CREATE CONTEXT THROUGH SYNTHESIS.

The French New Wave movie director Jean-Luc Godard quipped, "It's not where you take things *from*—it's where you take them *to*." Where you take them *to* is distinctive because of your uniqueness. The lens through which you process everything—your intake—creates an output that is a synthesis of your unique point of view combined with new information. This synthesis is what creates something new. Lin-Manuel Miranda created a universally acclaimed stroke of genius with *Hamilton: The Musical*. He transcended the genre of musical with innovative storytelling on American history through rap and hip-hop music and the lens of the under-represented. He reported that *Hamilton* was inspired by another Broadway hit, *Rent,* that preceded Miranda's masterpiece some nineteen years earlier.

Another element of synthesis is the information you take in. The more data points you can populate your mind with to synthesize, the more unique remixes and perspectives in problem solving and creation you will be able to generate. The more diverse those data points are to your perspective, the more you will open your mind to something new and novel, to you. Salvador Dali mused that

"KNOWING HOW TO LOOK IS A WAY OF INVENTING."

Keep changing and evolving the lens through which you synthesize the world, because new lenses are created by a continuously changing kaleidoscope of our perception, bias, and provenance.

THINKING. Your journey to possibilities need not include trying to be different. Many people equate originality with being different. That's not the case. Everything and everyone is derivative of someone or something else. Originality exists in *you:* in what interests *you*, in what moves *you*, in what compels *you*. Your one-in-a-trillion expression of something that resonated with you (for an unnamed reason too complex to dissect) is originality defined. Follow what catches your eyes, heart, and mind. And then, without regard to originality, create without consideration or judgment and see where you land.

LOOK FOR INSPIRATIONS EVERYWHERE, AND USE YOUR ONE-OF-A-KIND MIND TO BRING THEM TO NEW HEIGHTS.

DOING: 180-DEGREE FLIP. The ability to see something new in something old can come from simply tilting your head. With a simple head tilt, the slight shift in your orientation may cause you to notice a detail or idea that you had overlooked. Or create new and distinct data points to synthesize by turning your lens upside down. This simple flip works because it disorients your familiarity and opens up your perceptions, helping you come up with a ton of unique ideas. This is a simple shortcut to creativity. No stroke of genius is required. It's a great way to get out of your head.

Grab a pen and a piece of paper. Look around the room and pick up any common object.

On the piece of paper, list the object's characteristics and describe its properties.

Scissors: sharp, use with hands, cuts, metal . . .

Now next to each of those words, write a word with the opposite meaning. You should have two lists of words now.

sharp—dull
hands—feet
cut—attach

Looking at only the list of opposite words, try to sketch what the resulting object looks like. What image comes to mind with the new set of opposite characteristics?

Pretend you have to pitch this new object to a decision maker. Give it a name and describe what it does and how it works.

This activity is adapted from a similar one that Klutz publishing founder and d.school lecturer John Cassidy runs in our class. It's simplified here so you can do it by yourself quickly. In his original activity, students are given an excerpt of the familiar fairy tale *Cinderella* and asked to flip as many facets of the story's character, objects, intention, and scenario as they can and list these alternate possibilities. From that list they then assemble and present a new classic tale. The carriage becomes a holographic saucer, the princess becomes a social media obsessed teenager, and so on. The outputs are often laugh-cry worthy! I highly recommend doing this with a friend or two; share what you each come up with to exponentially increase the bounty of new concepts and details.

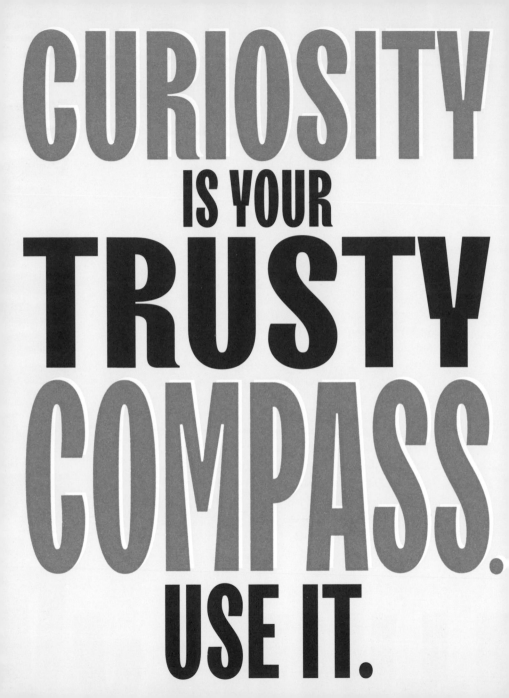

THE CURIOSITY CURE

KNOW YOU DON'T KNOW. Imagine that what you know fits inside a circle. And what you don't know is represented by the circumference of the circle. As you expand your knowledge base and your circle enlarges, the circumference also enlarges. The more you know, the more you realize you don't know. Further, you don't know what you don't know. This may be obvious, but sometimes we pretend to know, or worse, think we know. Both are very unproductive. It's okay to not know! In fact, it's fantastic, because you can only expand yourself from the place of not knowing.

Never mistake information for knowledge. Too often people erroneously equate information with knowledge or wisdom. Information is something you watch, hear, or read; knowledge comes from experience. Albert Einstein put it exactly like that: "Information is not knowledge. The only source of knowledge is experience. You need experience to gain wisdom." Information synthesized turns into knowledge—which, when activated, turns into wisdom. So to recap, from the bottom up: our inputs can go from information to knowledge to wisdom if we activate them properly.

BE CURIOUS ALL THE WAY. Not knowing and curiosity go hand in hand. Curiosity is essential to learning because it leads you to something you didn't previously know. And learning allows us to do better and better work. The more you learn, the more opportunities you can create. So follow your nose! Following your curiosity is like finding the end of a tangled ball of yarn and instead of snipping it loose, patiently and methodically untangling it. That's what Sirius XM radio cofounder Dr. Martine Rothblatt did when her young daughter was diagnosed with a rare incurable pulmonary arterial condition. She relentlessly researched the condition for a way to save her daughter's life. In the footnote of an obscure journal, she found the tip of a string in the form of a single molecule related specifically to her daughter's condition, which had failed in a medical trial. Rothblatt kept following her insatiable curiosity, and that led to the development of a new drug that saved not only her daughter's but thousands of other lives. In the process, it also created a billion-dollar industry for this specific medication.

Set aside your ego; embrace the courage to say, "I don't know," and expand from a position of not knowing. Knowing that you don't know is fertile ground for curiosity to flourish.

PURSUE WITH PURITY. I hold deep admiration for people like Dr. Rothblatt who are driven from their core to their calling or practice. Their entire existence is a living possibility, in a way so pure and seemingly beyond daily life chores: an artist who paints because they cannot imagine doing anything else, a scientist who keeps testing even after countless failed experiments. While that kind of dogged perseverance may be impractical for many of us, it's quite admirable—these people are standing in their utmost power because they are driven by curiosity and passion. At this intersection, we sing from our soul, a true expression of human spirit and the source of all creativity. This is where your purpose (heart) aligns perfectly with your actions/work (mind). It is a place of strength.

Moving from a place of curiosity can imbue your project with a certain potency that provides a clearer path to realizing your possibility. One of the great poets, e.e. cummings, clarifies this concept: "Once we believe in ourselves we can risk curiosity, wonder, spontaneous delight or any experience that reveals the human spirit." The confidence to take a risk leaves room for opportunity and wonder. We don't have to be the next Thomas Edison to impact the world. Margaret Mead, a renowned cultural anthropologist who was awarded the Presidential Medal of Freedom, said it best: "Never doubt that a small group of thoughtful, committed citizens can change the world; indeed, it's the only thing that ever has."

THINKING. Curiosity is your creative immune system. It helps you respond naturally to the hardship, surprises, and confusion that come with any creative or novel effort. It will help your ideas survive the difficult moments while making sure that you and your possibility or goal are aligned. When these two things are matched up, the path to realization emerges organically. All of us will suffer through things large or small, now or later—it's a universal truth. As you continue to be curious and open to learning more, you will naturally figure out the best next move and lead yourself down a good path.

FOLLOW CURIOSITY WITH INTENTION, AND WITHOUT EGO OR ASSUMPTION,
TO ALIGN YOUR HEART AND ACTIONS.

DOING: CURIOSITY COMPASS. Writing down what makes you tick (seeing a raucous concert, marveling at the height of an impossibly tall tree, walking your elderly neighbor's dog, holding the first physical prototype of a new project) can help you set an internal compass and remind you where, why, and how to explore the world. By taking a moment to capture things that excite you, you exercise self-perception, a first step to exercising your ability to set goals for yourself to achieve the unachievable. You also tap into the positive emotional state that these moments provide. This reflective activity should be done periodically. As we form and evolve as people, our point of view may also evolve and change. A curiosity compass is a great recalibration tool to have in anyone's personal development arsenal.

Using an 8½ by 11 sheet of paper, free write on one side. Recall momentous times or highlights of your life when you felt extremely happy, engaged, or excited, and write those down. Also capture what gets you excited. What are you passionate about?

2

Look over what you just captured.
Try to find four themes or emerging
patterns on the page. Summarize
what those are.

3

Flip the page over. Now encapsulate
the energy from your brainstorm
into a simple diagram with two axes
with four points (N-S-W-E) like
a compass. Plot the four themes on
the four points in any adjacency that
feels right.

Populate the compass with some of your current and future projects and possibilities. These are things that you want to do, learn, accomplish. This is your curiosity compass.

In class, we run a simpler version of this activity: using the output from Step 1, participants write a mission statement, encapsulating their sense of purpose in a single sentence. When everyone takes a turn to read theirs aloud in front of the class, it's declarative, affirmative, and very inspiring. I highly recommend doing either version of this exercise once a year and keeping a log of these personal compasses. Being able to go back to review what you thought and what you were setting your sights on in that moment is a thoughtful way to reflect on your path and progress. Undoubtedly, you will see patterns and possible trajectories that are only obvious in hindsight.

BE HONEST WITH YOURSELF ABOUT WHAT YOU WANT TO DO AND WHY YOU WANT TO DO IT.

CLARITY AND CONTEXT ARE POWER

BE AWARE OF EACH DEGREE. Not being clear on the reasons behind your possibilities is dangerous, because if you're slightly off course at the onset, the course correction later may be too significant to recover. It could put you in a situation that is difficult to change, expensive to redress, and challenging to reverse. This idea can be found in air navigation's 1 in 60 rule, which states that every 1 degree flown off course will result in 1 mile off course for every 60 miles flown. The longer you stray from the course, the farther you will be from your intended destination. That little 1 degree may seem immaterial in the first quarter mile traveled, but it can have a monumental impact on resources, time, destination, and safety by the hundredth mile. A quick d.school case study may help illustrate this point. Imagine you are helping a doctor in the developing world to save newborn babies' lives. He requests that you solve for a cheaper incubator, because incubators save babies' lives. His facility only has two, and he cannot afford more. If you blindly follow his request without getting a better understanding of how babies are served in his hospital, you'd miss the critical fact that most babies in that area don't make it to the hospital because they are born in rural areas too far away. While it's true that incubators are expensive and save babies, you would have spent resources chasing a solution that would not even touch the real issue that would save these babies' lives: providing a way for the mother to keep her baby warm after birth because she lives too far from a hospital.

GET YOUR INTENT STRAIGHT. Your original intent is the essence of any possibility. This basic intent, when held in place, anchors your effort. This is important because a funny thing happens when you get started on your project or product—you get embroiled in the minutiae. Little details creep up that you never knew existed and demand time you didn't allocate. You start feeling squeezed by the real pressures of financial obligations, operational logistics, and delivery timelines, an endless litany of necessary concerns such as estimated tax filings. You get so far removed from the spark of your fire that you become a bellows instead of the torchbearer. Though making your possibility a reality takes being *both* the bellows *and* the holder of the spark of your idea, it can feel monotonous and less exciting to be the bellows rather than the torchbearer. But things will be easier if you can remember why you started. If you do, the work is no longer a series of tasks; it becomes a way of being. You have to embrace the hard work and less fun tasks like number crunching in order to reach your outcome. The way to any amazingly cool outcome inevitably includes a pile of crap. For your possibilities, you get to pick your crap! Nothing good comes without it, it's part of the deal—so just own it.

FOCUS THE HEAT. Focusing on one possibility is sometimes clearly the right course of action. By working on fewer things, you are able to focus your attention and energy. Have you ever started a fire with a magnifying glass? A magnifying glass sets fire to tinder when it focuses the heat from strong overhead sunlight into a small concentrated point, created by sunlight passing through the convex glass. The smaller the point, the more concentrated the heat. If the concentrated point of heat is focused long enough on dry material like straw, it ignites. Imagine if your pursuit or possibility is that dry tinder you want to set aflame, and your focus is the point of light. If you are distracted or unfocused, the energy is too diffused, and your project will have a harder time catching fire. If the energy is focused, the fire will ignite, and it will spread infectiously.

There are a handful of prioritization frameworks out there used by consultants and user experience designers, but one quick way to help you gain focus is through constraint. When you reduce the number of variables of your concern, there's less to contemplate, and you can arrive more quickly at your desired outcome. I like to use "need to have" versus "want to have" as a starting point to focus. For example, when my belongings were stolen during a backpacking trip abroad, I learned that all I really need when I travel is my current outfit, a toothbrush, and a change of underwear. How's that for traveling light? What does your project *really* need?

DRAW THE SHAPE AROUND THE SHAPE. What you want to do is as important as what you don't want to do. What it *isn't* is as important as what it *is*. I'll never forget my first painting class at Berkeley. That's where I learned that there is neither foreground nor background, neither positive nor negative space. In a composition, there is only the object and the surround. To enforce this concept, we would step outside the studio and sit near the ivy beds, tasked to draw tendrils of ivy that run wild on the exterior of the art building. The constraint was that we were not allowed to draw the leaves themselves, but instead draw the shapes around the leaves because shapes shape other shapes. Everything surrounding the something you are drawing is as important and defining as the primary subject. Those surrounding shapes give the primary subject form. In order to focus, context is critical. Another great example that demonstrates this concept is the gradient illusion.

A uniformly gray bar sits squarely in the middle of a gradient field of gray that shades from dark to light horizontally. The part of the gray bar with the lighter-toned surround looks darker than the same gray bar with the darker-toned surround. We know the bar is the same tone on both sides, but the visual looks like a gradient-toned bar versus a solid-toned one. Context here is king. Don't let nonessential context distort your priority.

THINKING. Having a clear purpose and retaining clarity is important. Knowing and nurturing your purpose will keep your efforts focused like that magnifying glass. Anchor yourself in why you started. If what you are doing is the same choice you would make if you could do anything, then you likely have a clear purpose.

NARROW THE FOCUS ON YOUR INTENTION AND PAY ATTENTION TO CONTEXT
IN ORDER TO FURTHER CLARIFY WHAT YOU WANT TO ACHIEVE.

DOING: THEN WHAT HAPPENS. At the d.school, design problems are problems of innovation—not aesthetics. When solving for something, you have to ask a bunch of questions to make sure you're solving for the right thing. Imagine a company spending a ton of money and time building a solution for the wrong problem. It's very important that you ask the correct questions so you can solve for the correct problem or objective.

This activity about framing is by Stanford Professor Bernie Roth, from his course "Designer in Society" and his book *The Achievement Habit*. It cuts to the chase quickly to ensure that you are asking the right question and solving for the right thing in your life. By doing this, you will quickly home in on the real problem and what you're really solving for.

1

Start with a problem. Something that has been keeping you up at night. Be sure it is personal to you, such as *Should I start my own business?* versus *global warming*. Write it down on a piece of paper.

Should I start my own business?

Ask yourself what it would do for you if you solved Problem A. Answer B is what it would do for you.

What would it do for me if I started that business? It would allow me to work on things I care about.

Next make Answer B the next question—what it would do for you if it solved Problem B? Answer C is what it would do for you.

What would it do for me if I worked on things I care about? It would give the time and conviction to help make the changes I want to see in the world.

4

Next make Answer C the next question—what it would do for you if you solved Problem C.

What would it do for me if I were able to focus on making positive change in the world? I would be living my values.

Keep going until you get to the core of what you are really solving for.

5

Look back at your list of problems. Which one stands out to you as the one that really needs to be addressed? (Usually it's not the first—too specific—or the last—too broad—but somewhere in the middle.) The big reveal is that there is a deeper consideration at play.

In the preceding example, is the real issue starting a business, working on things you care about, making the changes you want to see, or living your values? Perhaps if the example was carried out for a couple more steps, the possibility of finding a new career path would reveal itself to be the concern you should really solve for. Again, Professor Roth would be the first to tell you that most reasons are bullsh*t. If you took the first question at face value and didn't dig a little more, you would have missed the real problem you should be solving. Repeat as needed.

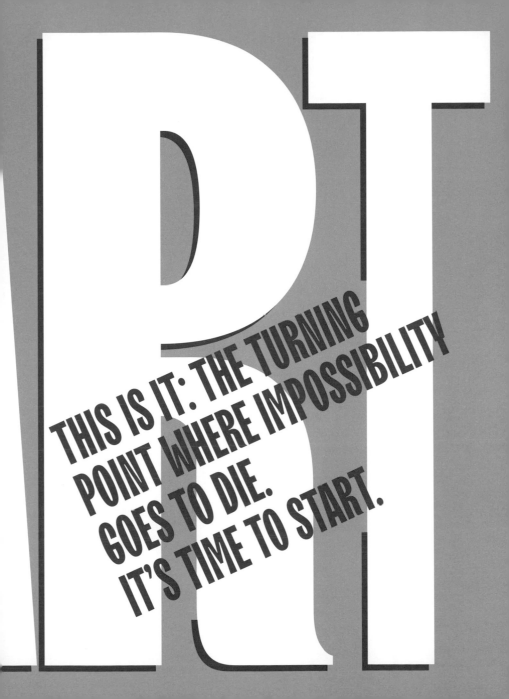

THIS IS IT: THE TURNING POINT WHERE IMPOSSIBILITY GOES TO DIE. IT'S TIME TO START.

Having the guts to begin is big. Starting is the line that divides action from inaction. It's so much easier to *think* about things than it is to actually *do* them. Pointing your skateboard down a ramp, starting a family, launching a business, going to school—doing *anything* for the first time—all can be daunting. The weight of the anticipation of what-ifs and the unknowns are way heavier than the actual act of doing or starting. It's sort of a weird phenomenon. A famous aphorism is, "Whatever you can do or dream you can, begin it. Boldness has genius, power, and magic in it!" Shed the mental burden by taking action. How you start is up to you. This section provides tips to get you going and to the other side of START.

TO START, CHOOSE WORK OVER WISH

Picture yourself in line at the grocery store at the end of day, when everyone is stopping in to pick up something for dinner. The line is moving slowly. A dad and his little kid are two feet in front of you. The child is pleading with the dad for the candy bar near the register. "Can I please get it? Why not? But I want it!" The whining voice escalates to an unbearable shriek. "It's not fair! I want it!"

This is what wanting looks like. At face value, it's frustrating to watch. The kid is so attached to the idea of getting the candy, they are oblivious to the spectacle they're creating. Wanting is the antithesis of making possibilities happen. What if the kid in the grocery store instead came up with something to do about it, a way to talk the dad into buying the candy bar—perhaps do more chores for it, offer to forfeit dessert at dinner, remind him about the good report card, or offer to pay for it with their allowance. To make possibilities happen, you need to replace wanting with working.

Instead of wistfully thinking of something you wish you could have or achieve, get up and do something about it—or forget about it. Thoughts don't become real without action. Yes, get up and get moving. I cannot emphasize this enough. A goal without work is just a wish. Turn your wishbone into a backbone.

GO: TURN THOUGHTS INTO ACTION.

TO START, HAVE A VISION, NOT AN EXPECTATION

Buddha said, "You only lose what you cling to." Although creating a detailed vision is crucial to realizing an idea (see chapter 2), and visualizing what it will feel like to have accomplished something is great, it is very different from being attached to a certain outcome.

When you become inseparable from your desired happy ending, you can turn your guiding vision into a burdensome expectation. That fixation can keep you from starting. Becoming attached may lead you to be inflexible toward other ways your vision can materialize. Or it can keep you from starting because you're so infatuated with the endpoint that you can become fearful that it will not materialize. And even if you do get started, attachment can keep you so married to a certain result that you miss a greater opportunity or solution to an even better outcome that may evolve while you are making things happen.

GO: BE CLEAR AND FLEXIBLE WITH YOUR VISION, NOT YOUR EXPECTATION.

TO START, DETACH FROM PROJECTED OUTCOMES

Another kind of attachment is living in fear of what you don't want to happen. The remedy? Remember, it's not the outcome that matters—it's the goals, the experience, and the process. The fruition of a goal could be an outcome, but there are many possible outcomes to that goal being achieved. We've all had thoughts like, *I'll be happy once I have this job, once I've solved that problem, once this goes to market.* This type of thinking is all too common. You attach to certain outcomes because of what you imagine these desired situations will bring you. As we examined in the Then What Happens activity on page 57, you may be confounding what you really need by projecting what a certain outcome will provide. Again, it's the experience and process, not the outcome, that matters. You will never walk away empty handed if you have this mindset.

The backstory of the invention of Post-it Notes illustrates this concept. In 1969 a scientist at 3M accidentally created a low-tack adhesive in his pursuit of a super-strong adhesive. He promoted it within the company for several years without any supporters, until his colleague Art Fry used it as a bookmark for his 1974 hymn book and resurfaced the project at the company. Even then, market test results were poor. It wasn't until its second market introduction in 1980, more than a decade after its creation, that the product caught on. This string of events shows that even if the outcome is not what you wanted, you can expand your possibilities. Pursue everything for passion, enrichment, or experience. Don't hang onto fixed outcomes; possibilities will emerge along the way. You are not your outcomes.

GO: BEGIN WITH PROCESS TO END WITH POSSIBILITY.

TO START, YOU MAY NEED TO MAKE TIME

Every moment is a *use it or lose it* situation. The only real moment is the present. Neuroscientist Abhijit Naskar explored this in great detail and came to this conclusion:

"Time is basically an illusion created by the mind to aid in our sense of temporal presence in the vast ocean of space. Without the neurons to create a virtual perception of the past and the future based on all our experiences, there is no actual existence of the past and the future. All that there is, is the present."

Time as we think of it (ticks on a dial), was created by humans more than 3,500 years ago to track the Earth's rotations on its axis and measure the day's passage. The science behind how time actually works is a rabbit hole worth diving into, but for the purpose of possibilities, time is not as clear-cut as we humans make

it out to be. Physicists since Albert Einstein have theorized that time may not work in the sequential ways it seems to us. Once you understand that our perception of time is varied, you can stop letting it drive you, and instead shape your perception to drive it.

According to Einstein, time is relative to your perspective. A good way to visualize this is in terms of light and shadow. If you put a small can of soda on a table and shine a flashlight directly at the can, it casts a very long shadow. If you shine the flashlight down on top of the can, it casts no shadow at all. Regardless of the shadow size, the can is still the same size. Time attaches itself to tasks like a shadow: the size of the task can grow or shrink depending on your perspective. Take your tasks out into the high noon sun and get them done.

GO: CREATE YOUR OWN CONSTRUCT OF TIME.

TO START, DON'T WAIT

We take so many things in our lives for granted, and among them time is a biggie. Here are some time-related obstacles you may be facing and ways to handle them. The key here is that waiting (and wanting) slows you down, while action speeds things up. Possibilities live in momentum. Turn waiting into doing with these Xs, Ys, and Zs.

Waiting "to get to X"? Try one of these:

- Do the things you'd do as if you already had X.
- Do an activity in an arena adjacent or related to X.
- Try doing something completely different—it may jar your thinking.

Waiting "to hear from Y"? Here are some ideas:

- Widen or deepen your field of vision by talking to other Ys.
- Go knock on other doors and start another ball rolling. Like fishing at a pier with multiple rods—why use only one to catch a fish?
- Sketch out other ways the outcome can happen and break down each of those ways into actionable steps. (Y isn't the only path to your desired outcome.)

Waiting "until Z is in place"? Some helpful tips:

- Know that the only "right" moment is the one in which you take action.
- Know that having an exhaustive, complete set of circumstances is impossible, so make the most informed decision you can in that moment, then move forward.

START
NOW
AND BE
PATIENT.

One more thing to keep in mind: Rome was not built in a day. In fact, it took 1,229 *years*. Moreover, it took 6,432 hours for you to physically come into existence, and that's pretty darn quick, given the complexity of the human body! Fact is, things take time. Moreover, things take longer than you think. Now is not only the right time to begin; now is the only time.

GO: START NOW AND BE PATIENT.

TO START, FIRST CHECK YOUR FEAR

Fear is one of the six universal human expressions that have no cultural boundaries. We all have the ability—and tendency—to imagine potential negative outcomes (see chapter 1). And that's the hitch. These fabricated thoughts—these things we *think* about—may keep us from even starting. Daniel Kahneman was awarded a Nobel Prize in Economics in 2002 for his work on the prospect theory, which demonstrates people's tendency to accept outcomes that are certain—even if it's a certain loss—rather than take larger risks even if they might pay. Our human aversion to loss and our need for certainty is easily demonstrated by the multi-billion-dollar insurance industry. The known expense of insurance is often favored over an unknown potentially greater expense if something unfortunate were to occur. This can be applied to your projects. Don't let your thoughts keep you from starting. Don't accept the current "lesser" loss of the existing situation.

GO: CONSIDER YOUR RISKS BUT DON'T OVER-INDEX POTENTIAL NEGATIVE OUTCOMES.

TO START, AIM YOUR ATTENTION

We know we're prone to focus on the negative. We know thoughts direct energy. We also know that it's important to pay attention to our attention. To take that a step further, because your energy follows your thoughts, focus on things you believe in and you'll create possibilities. Don't focus on your fears or you'll attract them to you! Every time I have focused on fear, the outcome has been subpar or detrimental. Unless safety is at stake, don't base decisions on fear, because when you do, you are usually making a decision in fear of something bad (negative) versus making a decision for something you hope to bring to life (positive). You are making a decision in

reaction to a potential negative outcome that may or may not happen. Doesn't that sound irrational when you hear it like that? Franklin D. Roosevelt said, "The only thing we have to fear is fear itself." Later, he went on to elaborate that it is "nameless, unreasoning, unjustified terror" that keeps us from advancing. When you can practice acting out your desired behavior in moments of discomfort, you are learning to say "Hi" to your fears, so you can wave them to the exit.

GO: ACT TOWARD DESIRED OUTCOMES NOT FEARED ONES.

TO START, RESPOND VERSUS REACT

Starting something new can be stressful. But just as you can base big decisions on hopes (buying a house one day) instead of fears (staying in miserable job without exploring other possibilities for fear of losing your home), you can train yourself to *respond* to smaller, in-the-moment decisions thoughtfully instead of *reacting* emotionally. A response characteristically comes about more slowly than a reaction. It is made with regard to a desired outcome in mind, so it's usually positive. A reaction usually happens quickly as a defense mechanism and leaves the outcome, positive or negative, to chance.

A famous 1962 experiment by Seymour Levine showed that infant rats responded more effectively to novel situations after being exposed to intermittent foot shocks compared to rats that did not receive any shocks. This "stress/ fear inoculation" indicates that a little bit of stress or fear is good in small consistent doses; it can help develop an enhanced resilience and tolerance to stress. This means we can create some immunity to fear and uncertainty by slowly exposing ourselves to situations that are uncomfortable. Physiologically, our bodies adapt, much like how we can reduce allergic reactions with small, controlled exposures to the allergen. Emotionally, little things like eating at a new restaurant or taking a different route on your commute home may feel imbalanced at first, but quickly become comfortable— after all, every good friend started off as a stranger. It also shows that through practice we can be better responders. Freedom comes from the ability to respond, to act consciously, with consideration beyond the immediate information at hand.

60: CONDITION YOURSELF INTO BEING A GOOD RESPONDER.

Every action can be classified as a beginning, the start at the front of all the doing that follows. Like the fabricated frameworks of time we learned about, the transition from starting to doing does not have to be a fixed sequence to make possibilities happen. In fact, if you ever feel like you're spinning your wheels when you DO, just pop back here to START for a little bit, then begin again.

IN THE FACE OF REJECTION, FAILURE, AND THE SH*T STORM OF THINGS THAT ARE OUT OF YOUR CONTROL, HOW DO YOU MAINTAIN MOMENTUM?
ANSWER:
TAKE ACTION AND DO. THAT'S IT. NOTHING HAPPENS WITHOUT DOING.

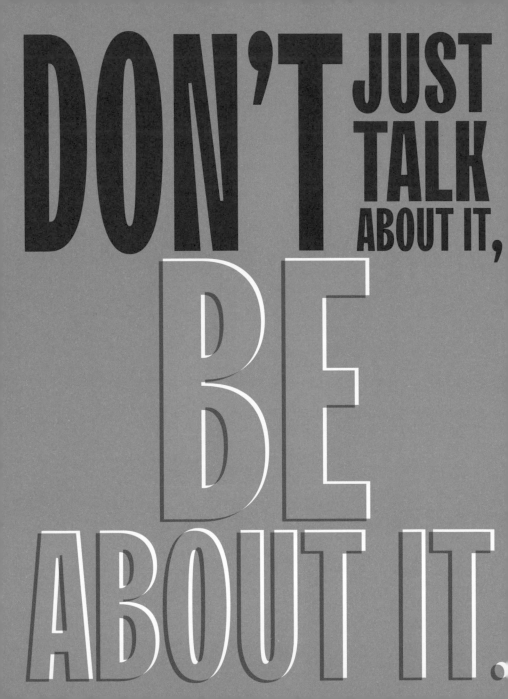

7 IDEAS VERSUS EXECUTION

TURN IDEAS INTO ACTION. An idea is the starting point of your possibility in the form of an abstract concept, vague notion, or formulated thought. There is a limitless supply of ideas in this world. Everyone seems to have a million great ideas. Applying the microeconomic theory of supply and demand, ideas hold little value because they are in endless supply. The ideas floating in people's heads are like all those middle school crushes you romanticized from afar. Let's get real: did you ever do anything about those? What *is* in short supply are people with the courage to act on their ideas (or crushes). Ideas translated into action—that's where value creation begins because action is what changes the supply-and-demand curve. Action creates value.

Earlier in the book we talked about how information alone holds no value, but information distilled, synthesized, and activated creates knowledge and wisdom. *Doing* doesn't depend on competency or perfection. Doing is about transforming ideas into action. The more you do, the more you'll grow and learn.

SET YOUR IDEAS FREE. Ideas alone don't mean squat without a masterful execution. Remember the film *Big* with Tom Hanks? Back in 1988, it was a hit, racking up $151.7 million in box office receipts (equivalent to $354.7 million in 2021). In my graduate screenwriting class, a top talent executive explained that there were more than a dozen pitches with a story similar to *Big* prior to the creation of the blockbuster film. So the idea for the movie *Big*—"After wishing to be made big, a teenage boy wakes the next morning to find himself mysteriously in the body of an adult"—was not unique. The value came from the execution. First the writer wrote the script. Then there's the cast, the director, the editing—the list goes on. The variety in execution you can get out of the standard 120-page script for a ninety-minute film is almost infinite. The point is that a masterful execution is like a needle in a haystack, a perfect storm of infinite variables culminating in value creation. There is little value in a simple story idea, but when you take action on the idea, it can transform into a rare gem.

GIVE FORM TO CONCEPT. An undeveloped idea is a formless starting point, just like a lump of clay thrown on the potter's wheel. To become something useful, it needs a potter's influence. Once that lump of clay begins to spin, the height and curvature of the walls are shaped by the hands of the potter. The form does not go from lump to vase in an instant; it evolves and emerges over time, guided by the potter's skill and vision. An idea takes shape like that lump of clay in motion. The vase does not result without the fluid working of the clay. One step informs the next. The working (execution) is what gives the vase viability (value).

Every sequence of an idea's evolution is part of its transformation, turning an intention or concept into form and reality. The first step to action is to get your ideas out of your head and onto paper. When you free your idea onto the sheet, you give it form as a potter does to a lump of clay. When a compelling concept comes to me, I like to immediately capture it by jotting it down. I usually let it marinate in the back of my mind for a day or a week, then revisit it. If it is still compelling when I come back to it, that's a sign that the idea may have meaning or value, as part of another project or maybe an entirely new stand-alone pursuit.

Take any action immediately to evolve and build on your idea, whether it is jotting notes down or doing a little research on the topic. Every little bit of action or information you capture counts. Every input adds shape to the end result. Keep repeating the process and you'll find yourself with a curated collection of ideas in varying degrees of progression. I love surveying the gaggle of ideas and their progress.

THINKING. While ideas and purpose are the book cover of possibility, taking the first step is putting the first word on the first page. There is no book without a first page, just as there are no pages without the first word. To make a possibility real, we have to bring it into the world of action. Accomplishing one small task in service of your project will set it in motion. This can be jotting a note, saving a link to read later, making a sketch, or starting a list of tasks or facets to research. If you don't capture it while it is in your attention, you risk never remembering it. So seize the moment. Do that one small thing. Then do another small thing. And another. These little hustles will build the base of your possibility and give it momentum.

GIVE FORM TO IDEAS WITH AN ABUNDANCE OF ACTIONS THAT WILL ACCUMULATE INTO VALUE. IDEA TO FORM, FORM TO SHAPE, SHAPE TO EXECUTION.

DOING: OUTTA YOUR HEAD. An idea log is not just a place to jot down ideas, but a place to work them out. Look at it, doodle on and around it, as that can inspire other ideas or allow you to see important facets new to your idea. Never erase anything—your work shows your thought process. Keep these outputs. Even if it ends up being something you do not use (this time), it may be part of something in the future. You'll be amazed to see how you synthesize all your bits over time. What you'll find is that the log becomes a physical representation of your mental sandbox.

1

Get a system to write or draw things down. Any repository will do, analog or digital. I toggle among three instruments: a 5 by 7 paper journal of fifty blank pages, multiple digital slide files, and digital notes organized by project.

2 Fill your repository with your inklings, thoughts, inspiration, images, and ideas as they arise. It can be both a record of random bits and the worktable to grind out some ideas. It can be questions you are wondering about or something you cannot finish processing at the moment.

3 Instead of making entries only when struck with lightning, try to make your idea log a daily discipline, and watch it become part of your arsenal.

The repository you create for your musings will work best if you can access it anytime, anywhere. Setting up project folders that can retain a variety of media is a good way to organize. I often take photos of tangible artifacts, such as tear sheets or analog notes, to easily access and catalog. I also have a front-burner folder for active projects and a back-burner folder for inactive projects. (Yes, that unfinished screenplay from grad school is still in the back-burner folder!) Regardless of which method works for you, your vault will collect precious gems in various raw, cut, or polished forms.

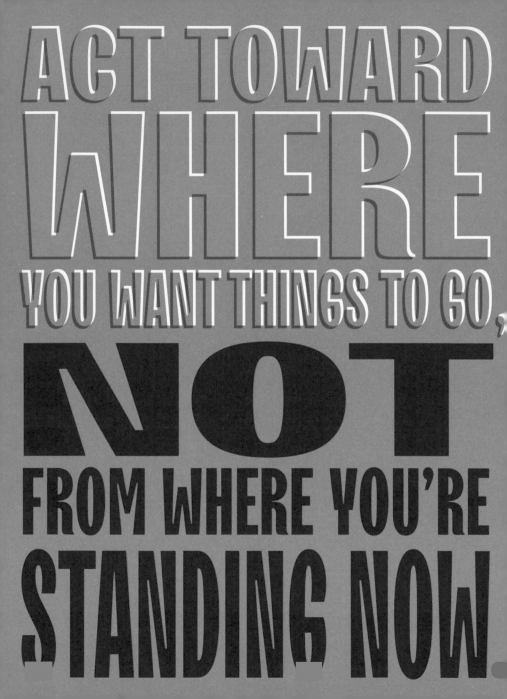

8 PROACTIVITY RULES

CREATE ENERGY WITH ACTION. While energy itself is invisible, we can see what happens when it gets applied. Energy can be transformed into almost any state, like ice into water, water into vapor. It can create temperature change and momentum, and it can advance things through progress and refinement. Nothing happens without energy. Action creates energy, but if your actions aren't mindful, you'll be wasting it. Think of pumping up a bicycle tire. If you don't secure the pump nozzle to the fill attachment on the tire properly, you can hear the fruits of your labor escape as you pump. You may even be letting out more air than you are putting in! Complete each action one at a time with intention. Every step in this process matters. Repeated behaviors become habits, and by taking action you develop a dependable go-to response for any possibility.

I have an action-oriented habit expertly honed from my very Pavlovian upbringing. As a young child, I was precluded from roller skating with my neighborhood friends until I had finished homework, house chores, and, yes, piano practice. I have transformed this work-before-play mentality into a clear bias to action in developing ideas or solving problems. I realized that the more I did, the more things I could get done. Doing is like an electric charge to my battery. Action provides me with more energy and power rather than depleting them.

THINK LESS, DO MORE. Physical action is critical to any creative work—when you work out ideas *outside* of your head, you are what the d.school calls "building to think." Our scientific study at Stanford on creative capacity building supports this. For the study, we provided participants with a multifaceted word like *salute* and asked them to draw an expression of the word. We assessed the creativity of the drawings based on the fluency (number of elements), originality (uniqueness of concept), elaboration (extent of details), representation (intelligibility), human centeredness (empathy), and closure (completeness of overall expression). The data from the fMRI brain scans showed that the *less* the participants thought about what they were drawing, the more creative their drawings were. This shattered the expectation that the prefrontal cortex, usually tied to thinking, would be more active.

The creativity training sessions for the research subjects were short, time-constrained conceptual activities that incorporated a lot of physical prototyping tasks. The study results also showed that after participants underwent creativity training, the part of the brain that is usually associated with movement was more active in the higher-ranked creativity tasks. The study participants' action-oriented behavior was the crux of their transformations. If you think less and do more, the outcomes you produce will likely be more creative.

THROW A LEADING PASS. Sports provide great metaphors for possibilities. Just like the flow of our daily lives, athletes are always in motion. In many games like football, soccer, or lacrosse, an instrumental way to advance toward the goal is to throw a leading pass: one thrown to where the moving receiver will be when the pass arrives, not to where the receiver is standing at the moment the ball is thrown. It's important to note that every player on the field is usually on the move in intentional ways. If the person with the ball stops to throw versus throwing on the move, they risk losing possession as a sitting duck target for the opposing team's defense. If the receiver stops to catch the ball, they risk losing possession for the same reasons. The lesson: Always stay in motion when passing or catching the ball, figuratively. Hockey great Wayne Gretzky famously said, "Some people skate to the puck. I skate to where the puck is going to be."

Apply this to how you work toward your possibilities— make decisions in a forward motion. A good example can be found in marketing and advertising. When the objective is to expand the customer base or sell a product, you design strategies that target the customer base you are shooting for in volume and type, not necessarily to the customer base you already have. Focus on the direction you want to go—which is toward the goal, not where you are currently standing.

FLOW LIKE WATER. Along the way, things are bound to get between you and what you are trying to create. Something's not working as anticipated? Make an adjustment. Something unexpected arises that obliterates your assumptions? Recast the assumptions and check the objective. An often-used metaphor for this concept is the river and the rock, succinctly expressed by Bruce Lee when asked about his fighting philosophy: "Be like water." A river flows around stationary rocks en route to the ocean. Over time, the water wears the unyielding rock down to a pebble. Choose to be the flexible river, not the stationary rock, and use gravity to help carry you to the end goal.

When prototyping the user interface in the early stages for Paper Punk, an origami-meets-LEGO paper block construction toy, we wanted to eliminate the need for scissors or glue in making a fully enclosed block. We manufactured a convenient pull-strip adhesive in prototype form. After we delivered the final files, the factory quickly reported back that using multidirectional adhesive in mass production was impossible without building bespoke machinery—which we couldn't afford. Finding out there was no way to make our original idea work forced us to rethink the whole product. It was no fun in the moment, but it opened up an entirely new direction that we never would have considered. Our solution was an adhesive-free tab and notch system that allowed the paper blocks to be double sided—an added feature not possible with the initial pull-strip interface, which only utilized one side of the blocks. Coming up against a hard obstacle pushed us to get creative to move around it. It forced us to be the river, not the rock.

THINKING. Nothing happens unless you do something about it. This is the fundamental law of inertia. You may be deflated from a setback, exhausted from working, or perhaps even elated from some kind of wonderful thing that's happened. However, none of that matters. To bring things to life, you still have to show up and do the work. You show up because your heart compels you to, in spite of and despite all of the things that may color your mood or productivity. Great work is in the doing. Doing is the discipline and habit that transforms ideas into possibilities and makes progress possible.

SHOW UP EVEN IF YOU DON'T FEEL LIKE IT, AND GET TO WORK.

DOING: 3-15-60 MINUTES. Use self-imposed time constraints to turn habits into productivity. In the test subject training of our creativity study just mentioned, we exposed participants to multiple timed activities that transformed their creative thinking. This activity builds from that same concept. Time constraints are very generative because they force you to focus. The time frames, selection, and crossing out completed tasks are all intentional aspects of this habit-building activity. Let's be honest: you can easily vaporize the same amount of time looking at social media! Lose the self-loathing of time wasted. Practice being productive.

1 Take a task you've been putting off. Make a list of items that would advance it to completion.

2 Categorize them as best you can into how long each task will take to complete: 3, 15, or 60 minutes.

3 Circle two 3-minute tasks and complete them right now. Cross them out.

4

Now circle a 15-minute task and do it. When it's completed, cross it out.

5

Keep shuffling and prioritizing your tasks by time chunks. This is a live, moving list. You should be adding items to this list and deleting them according to *time needed to complete* and *priority*.

These lists not only give you structure, but also validate what you achieved and free up space in your mind by getting all those tasks out of your head. Most people procrastinate on larger tasks. To avoid that, break down the larger task to smaller, less daunting ones.

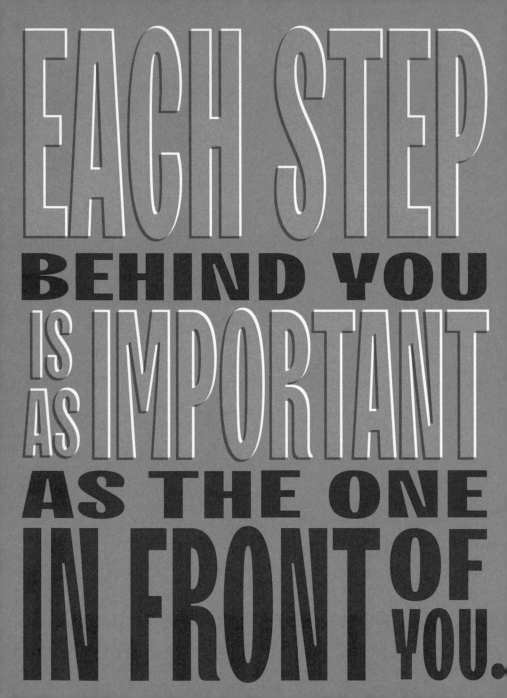

9 THE LADDER PRINCIPLE

SEE THAT SEQUENCE MATTERS. Execution isn't doing just a few things—it's doing some very specific things, usually in a specific order and even in a particular way. Consider when you climb a ladder to get on top of your roof, do you go rung by rung or do you skip rungs as you occasionally do on stairs? What happens if you skip rungs on a ladder when you descend? Is the stability of the ladder the same if you were to go one by one versus skipping a rung? What other factors do you think impact the climb up or down—sequence, speed, hand placement, foot order, confidence, grip strength? Which part of your foot rests on the rung? When you really break it down, the nuances of climbing up or down a ladder are more complex than you might care to think about.

The crux of the ladder principle is that there are no shortcuts. Imagine a ladder with only a bottom and top rung—how useful would it be for getting onto a roof? Each rung is analogous to the progression of your potential project. Do one thing to completion and you will feel good about it. Repeat it and it becomes a habit, a good habit. You will be up your ladder before you know it!

LEARN TO PASS THE BALL. Being an entrepreneur inevitably gives rise to feeling the need to clone yourself. There is always too much to do and not enough resources. A common trap is the feeling of *I can do it better/faster so I will just do it myself.* The problem comes when you multiply that decision by a thousand. Suddenly the time you supposedly saved is gone, and you are buried, stressed, and even more behind. Even though letting others take over some items in your domain is challenging, there is more growth ahead when we let go and allow others to take responsibility. Building on the leading pass example from the last chapter, I remember my college lacrosse coach reminding the team that a passed ball can travel faster than any one of us could run while carrying the ball. To advance the ball toward the goal more quickly, we needed to pass the ball more frequently.

As a serial entrepreneur, this is a lesson I keep learning. The first and last time I registered a trademark myself was not a good experience. We were trying to conserve resources and were on budget. I took on the task and successfully filed our mark, or so I thought. Moving ahead, we printed our branded demos and marketing materials with our logo and started taking meetings with the Sony Corps of the world. To our surprise, about six months later an article in the *New York Times* mentioned our trademarked name, but the article wasn't about us. Turns out a legacy music label had gone to press and market with our registered name without doing a trademark search. My lack of legal expertise had left a loophole in our filing and put our ownership of the mark in jeopardy. We lost the mark, to our great expense. My lesson learned: Know when to pass the ball.

LOVE THE DOING. An unattributable adage that I remind my kids of regularly is:

"HOW YOU DO ANYTHING IS
HOW YOU
DO EVERYTHING."

This means being mindful during all tasks, whether mundane or engaging. To me, this is fundamentally about not wasting your life, about getting into the habit of doing your best. Like making your bed—it takes the same amount of time to do a crappy job as it does to do an excellent job. Why spend the same time and have a messy bed? There are no shortcuts, and sequence matters. You have to put on the fitted sheet before you place the pillows! It takes what it takes. And not only that, the quality of your project relates to the amount of effort and emotion you put into it. So, love the doing, love the process.

THINKING. For a product designer, bringing a product to market represents the multitude of decisions that bring the object to fruition. And even if you're not designing something as complex as a rocket to Mars, some claim that the average adult makes thousands of decisions per day to a tune of about thirty-six decisions every waking minute, assuming you get eight hours of sleep. Every detail is a decision and, in summation, the details make the product, project, event, outcome—even your life. Get adept at making decisions, and you won't get bogged down by the multitude of choices.

MAKE THE
BEST DECISION
WITH THE INFORMATION AT HAND
IN THE MOMENT
AND MOVE ON.

DOING: MICRO MAP. Use Micro Mapping to quickly frame up the elements, steps, and sequence to make something happen. Think of this as a living to-do list that helps you to consider your approach, effort, and strategy to help achieve the desired outcome. By illuminating these elements on paper, you can quickly spot holes, new opportunities, and alternative ways of reaching your goals. If possible, do this with analog or digital sticky notes. This will allow you to move elements around and expand areas that require more steps. Carefully consider their sequence to create a plan of action. When you collect new info while you are executing a step, you may need to edit, add, or adjust what comes next. Expand and contract as needed. Consult this micro map periodically to keep from wandering.

1

On a sheet of paper, write out your *possibility* or *goal* as the headline. Below it you will be making a list.

2

First, write a *must-have element* to achieve that goal. Below that, write down two or three items you must do to achieve your goal. Repeat until you have several core must-haves.

> *Goal:* Print-on-demand side hustle
> *Must-have elements:* digital storefront, designs, print provider
> *Must-do for storefront:* register platform, buy URL, design interface

3 Now working horizontally, alongside the first element, note two or three *must-do* things to put that element in place. Do this for your remaining elements. The resulting map contains the action components you are aware of right now that could bring you closer to climbing the ladder and realizing your vision.

Micro mapping is a great way to chart a path, to spot potential hang-ups in advance, and to find solutions to those hang-ups. Ideally, organize a running list of to-dos under one larger task (such as building a digital storefront), moving the things you've accomplished to the end of the running list and keeping the next priority at the top. Seeing everything you've done to get to where you are will boost both your confidence and energy, because you'll marvel at all that you've already accomplished. I like to use a master cloud-based spreadsheet to track multiple projects this way on a weekly basis.

10 TENSION AND MOMENTUM

FLY AT YOUR ZENITH. I have an unscientific hypothesis: Tension is an essential ingredient for potent creative outcomes. I formed this hypothesis in grad school when I was working on a night shoot for a major studio. On the movie set there were some Academy Award winners in key roles. During production, the conventional wisdom is that you want things to go smoothly, because anything but smooth means delays, problems, budget overruns, and angry studios. However, a curious phenomenon arose. Whenever creative tensions arose on the set (between director and director of photography, director and actor, producer and director—anyone!), the scene came out better. The seasoned assistant director confirmed this theory with a laundry list of movies he worked on where high tension on set was correlated with box office success. Although this is just my hypothesis, it makes sense if you take a macro view. Tension—conflict in this case—is natural to the constantly evolving variables in the making of a film. For example, the cast's performances unfold in real time as the director helps shape the characters they are creating. Everything is spontaneous and shifting. The creative work comes from the ways in which each person and part of the process reacts to the other. Recognizing and diving into these tensions is where the magic happens. That's where possibility lies—in how things unfold.

With any creative act, as with any relationship, there are opposites at play at all times. In the everyday context, we can point to light versus dark, happy versus sad, hot versus cold. In a Creative Gym session on navigating, I like to share an excerpt from former Nike CEO Mark Parker's journal. His journal had a hand-scribbled list of the tensions he held in balance for Nike: macro versus micro, quantitative versus qualitative, physical versus digital, top line versus bottom line, direct versus delegate, art versus science, to name several. These are not mutually exclusive pairs of words; they are tensions embodied in a decision, project, or business. Kites fly at their zenith with the most wind resistance. This air resistance actually helps stabilize the kite and lifts it up. It's more difficult to fly a kite in strong winds, so it's no surprise that when we encounter tensions it feels like something is wrong because it feels challenging and difficult. But tension is a wonderful signifier that something can be better.

When I first designed Foldmade—an eco-friendly, productivity-driven school and office supply line for a mass retailer—there was an inherent tension among three primary design goals: innovative, eco-friendly, and value driven. These three factors are not organically in alignment—in fact, they are far from it. Making a product out of plastic is a lot less expensive than paper, but it's not eco-friendly. We solved the challenge by leaning into the inherent tensions of the paper material, which led us to design innovative features that delivered on all three goals in the form of a pressboard binder with a patented expandable spine that can increase capacity when needed. Doesn't that help make tension a welcome dinner guest? Tension is a place where great things emerge, so set it a place at the table.

STAY IN MOTION. Tension, a condition of being strained or stretched, is instrumental to creating and sustaining some degree of forward motion. Momentum refers to the quantity of motion that an object has. We can correlate Newton's laws of motion to our path to possibilities. When we overlay physics on top of psychology, the laws of motion can inspire our thinking and guide our progress.

▶ **Newton's first law of inertia.** This is the classic, "objects in motion tend to stay in motion." Conversely, if nothing is happening to you, and nothing does happen, you will never go anywhere. Motion (or lack of it) cannot change without the application of force. This is why a sprinter can't reach their maximum speed instantly or abruptly halt after crossing the finish line. Applied as a metaphor for your work, this is an obvious one. Action begets action. Inactivity keeps you in the same place. Once you get moving, it will be easier to keep moving.

▶ **Newton's second law of mass and acceleration.** Force is equal to the change in momentum (mass times velocity) over time. The more force, the more acceleration. The harder you hit a ball with a bat, the faster it moves. This law is less widely known but is most critical for our possibilities. Applied to our behavior, the more energy you direct toward a particular goal, the more quickly you come closer to that goal. This also underscores the importance of keeping focus.

▶ **Newton's third law of motion.** This is the law of action and reaction. It states that for every action there is an equal and opposite reaction. Simply put, action and reaction play off each other. Sometimes the reaction will throw you off course; other times the reaction itself is exactly what you need to move ahead—like the way a helicopter's rotors create lift by pushing air down.

As applied to an oldie-but-goodie burgeoning project, we activated the laws of motion to launch *ReadyMade,* a national award-winning design magazine. The project was bootstrapped, underfunded, and launched during a recession, right after the first tech bubble had burst. But the laws of physics would not be denied, and the title attracted a groundswell of hardcore readers who resonated with our mission of reuse design and the resurgence of craft.

We could not internally generate the volume of content we needed—the editorial budget was nonexistent—so we called on our passionate readers to submit ideas for publication. They answered with a flood of inspired and outlandish projects. This was our (and the publishing industry's) foray into reader-generated content. The sheer volume of submissions we received from magazine fans created a force that kept the magazine on a trajectory we could not have built in a traditional way, and it launched a cultural movement we are still proud of to this day.

THINKING. Tension and resistance are a positive influence in creating your optimal outcome. While that may seem counterintuitive, embracing the tensions—thanks to physics—will aid your momentum.

EMBRACE AND EXAMINE ANY TENSIONS THAT ARISE

TO SEE WHAT DESIGN OPPORTUNITY IS BOTH HIDING AND HELPING YOU PROGRESS TOWARD YOUR POSSIBILITIES.

DOING: TENSION TOGGLE. Take a moment to pause and look at your tensions. This will help reveal new possible paths that the tensions create. Better yet, it will help you manage the inevitable stress created by the tensions themselves. Try to pinpoint and capture tensions that are specific to you. For example, rather than just work-life balance, list "twelve-hour work days versus having dinner with my family." By exposing the tensions and reflecting on them, you may be able to see how you can use them to your benefit and advantage. Acknowledge that having tension is okay and that the items in tension are not mutually exclusive. Missing family dinners because of work may signal that you need to establish better work schedule boundaries, establish better scheduling practices for yourself, or that maybe you are avoiding something at home. The main point here is to see the tension outside of yourself and to give it some thought. This will help ease the burden of the tension consciously and unconsciously.

1 Reflect on the different tensions you may have around the things you are trying to bring to fruition and what is in tension with them (work, family, relationships, beliefs, business ideas, and so on). Try to identify as many tensions as you can by writing them down.

2 Look at all the tensions and cluster them to see if there are any patterns or contradictions to the balance of these tensions. Some clusters may look like: *personal time versus professional demands; work versus family; work versus exercise*

> **Pattern:** *work appears to be impacting health, relationships, free time*

3 Notate some thoughts around the tension, like how it may be a positive or negative and the factors that drive it.

For an added benefit to writing down your tensions, apply the Serenity Sorting activity filter (see page 33). It may reveal that some of the concerns you hold in tension are not within your control. This does not mean you can cross them off the list, but it may assign them a different weight in your mind or may change that tension point to another, more productive or actionable item. It's okay to have tension, as long as you direct that force toward curiosity and action.

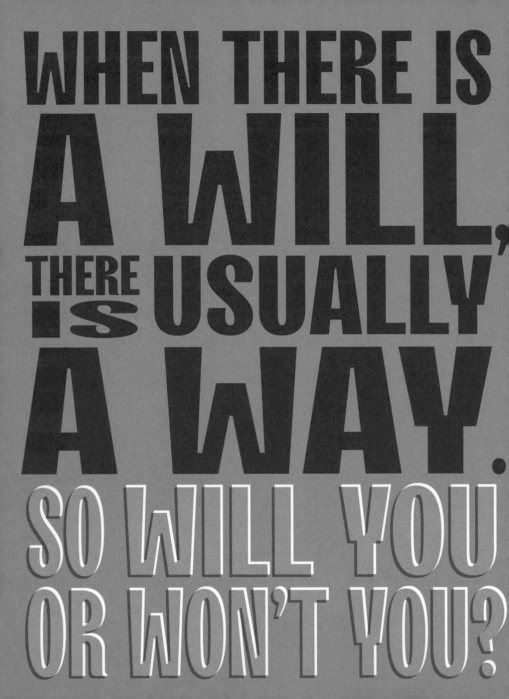

11

UNMARKED WAYS

FIND FOLLOW-THROUGH FROM COMMITMENT.
There are many ways to get something done, but
commitment creates staying power when facing challenges.
As I shared in the beginning of the book, the human brain is
hardwired to keep us safe. Safe means not taking a risk, and
it means holding back even a little, just in case. This self-
protection mechanism typically does not serve your projects,
goals, and possibilities positively.

Let's look at learning a new skateboard trick. Think of a
trick as a condensed version of one of your larger pursuits
where commitment is key to your success. A trick is a
condensed version because in mere seconds, the execution
of the trick has started and ended. You landed it, or you
didn't. A skater will tell you that despite understanding all
the nuances of executing the trick—even after breaking
it down and mastering all the mechanics to physically
execute it—it's really a mental game. When a skater is
having trouble landing a new trick, the reason is almost
always *you just need to commit.*

When you commit, you are more likely to push through,
even when a momentary reflex of self-protection tells you

not to. Our brains have sneaky ways of slipping in at the last minute to second guess ourselves and try to reduce risk on our behalf. Being 100 percent committed creates behavior usually associated with higher intelligence. Because humans are capable of self-reflection and reasoning, they are able to direct their attention, efforts, and energies with intention. Remember, to combat these trepidations, you need to fully commit before you leap.

CALL OUT THE NEED. As mentioned in the START section, misplaced desire can get in the way. Wallowing in wanting can stop you from working. I have a personal theory: vague desire thwarts action, but having real needs flips wanting into doing. I watched my parents work their tails off to make a living and build a life from scratch for their family. When they immigrated to the United States in their mid-twenties, they had no support system, either from their homeland or stateside. Everything they did and accomplished was because they had to; there was no safety net. Because of this, I cultivated an instinctive response—to take action. It's an inextricable part of my childhood and something I learned from watching them. Anyone can develop that instinct. While my parent's extrinsic needs may have been logistical, intrinsic need can be an equally powerful driver. I'm talking about the people who are driven by some indescribable inspiration—like the inventors, athletes, artists, educators, and others who seem to be answering a calling. In these cases, their need to *do* is the equivalent of breathing to survive. Identifying an extrinsic or intrinsic need can be a useful way to help you turn aspirations into action.

PUNCH UP YOUR WILL TO PERSIST. Will is a blood relative of commitment. Will is your capacity to decide what to do and when to act in resonance with your possibility and in spite of external influences. Your will enables you to keep working over a period of time, take deliberate action, persist in the face of adversity, and point your attention toward what you want to make happen in the world. We all have will, and we should call it to action again and again when we stumble.

I like using the metaphor of a house. When you enter your home, you usually go through the front door. Occasionally, you may enter through a back door or side door. Regardless, it's a door. What if you were locked out of every door? What other openings can get you from the outside of your home to the interior? Maybe you'd wait for someone with a key to open it. But what would you do if you left something cooking in the oven? Maybe you would check the windows or try slipping the lock open with a credit card. The stronger the will, the more ways you will find to gain access to the house.

Again, when launching *ReadyMade,* we cold-called Richard Hayne, the owner of Urban Outfitters, Anthropologie, and Free People, to ask him to be an angel investor. After all, he knew a lot about cultural cool, founding Urban Outfitters back in the 1970s, and his customers were our readers. When we tried tugging on his nostalgic heartstrings while extolling the virtues of *ReadyMade*, we could see our verbal assault making his eyes glaze over. We started losing him about halfway through the meeting, but knew we could not walk away empty handed. I asked if there was another way he could help us out—could he carry the magazine in his stores? He ended up not only committing to distributing *ReadyMade* in all his Urban Outfitters stores, but sharing his customer list with us. This was better than gold. Will is the corrective lens to production failure.

WHEN YOU HAVE AN INDESTRUCTIBLE WILL, YOU CAN FIND OPPORTUNITY IN FAILURE.

THINKING. Finding ways to realize your possibilities despite the obstacles that arise requires more than motivation. It requires desire, determination (associated with purpose), and persistence (associated with action). The stronger your will, the more likely you will find your way to what you need to move your project forward.

LISTEN TO YOUR WILL AND LET LOOSE—
IT WILL UNCOVER HIDDEN POSSIBILITIES FOR YOU.

DOING: GETTING TO THE ESSENCE. The will to discover is a skill you can build with practice. Use this activity to strengthen your ability to see possibilities. You can repeat it with different words and see how your mental agility evolves. This is especially fun if you do it simultaneously with other people. You can create variations of this challenge by changing the word. First start with simple tangible nouns (tiger), then progress to intangible nouns (love), adjectives (frustrated), and finally adverbs (frequently). Constraints in this activity are intentional for you to get creative and specific in how you express the respective word. Warning: This is very challenging.

1 Take a small memo pad with sheets that are about 3 by 5 inches.

2 Set a timer for 60 seconds. Write down any word of your choice— nouns, adjectives, and adverbs are all welcome.

3 Start your timer and flip the paper over. Create an image that expresses the essence of the word using only circle, square, and triangle shapes within the allotted time. You may use as many or as few of the shapes as you need for your drawing, as many times as you need. The time constraint will force you to not think too hard about what you will draw. The shape constraint will force you to really distill the essence of the word you are drawing.

4 Show your drawing to a friend and ask them what word they think of when they view your drawing.

5 Reveal the word and explain the essence of your drawing and why you used the shapes the way you did.

This activity forces you to drill down to the essence of a word and draw an expression of it with limited shapes—fortifying your ability to take something concrete and making it abstract in the most distilled way. This will come in handy when you are in the thick of anything and having a difficult time seeing your way out.

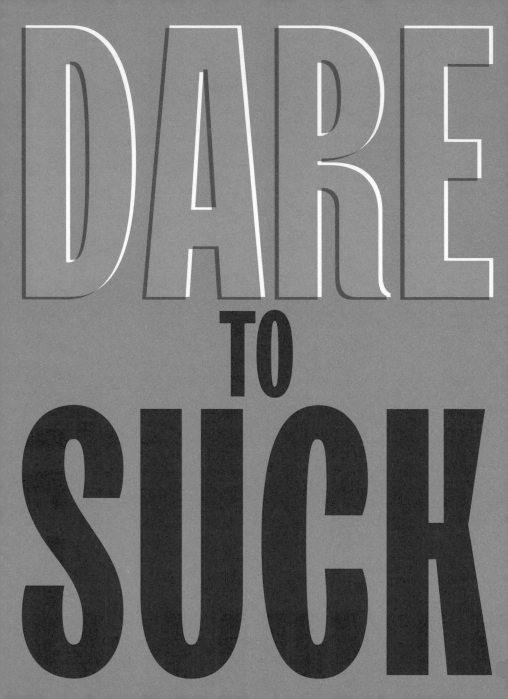

12
FORGET PERFECTION

FERTILIZE YOUR LIFE WITH FAILURE. Plants handle stress by adapting. When they undergo stress, their systems generate cellular responses that help create a tolerance for the stresses. That resistance translates into bigger blossoms, more fruit, and a healthier, more productive plant. Stress—and more specifically, failures— can fortify our projects in the same ways. In this regard, failure can be a good thing. It is just a data point indicating that you need to course adjust, not a scarlet letter on your chest. Anyone worth their salt will know that you need to fail in order to succeed. Steven Tyler of Aerosmith said, "That's how you write a song, too. You've got to put in ten stupid things if you want to get two great out. That's where it's at. Dare to suck. . . . There's the creativity. There's the childlike godness." Yes, it probably takes ten awful things to yield two great ones. If you're lucky.

PICK PROGRESS OVER PERFECTION. Perfection gets in the way of progress. I'm not suggesting you do the minimum viable amount of work, but I'm also not suggesting you wait to get it absolutely perfect, because it'll never be perfect. Get it done and move forward. A good plan today is better than a perfect plan tomorrow.

That said, launching imperfect things into the world, knowing they are harmful and not taking responsibility to correct something that isn't working, is a nonstarter, regardless of whether you began with good intentions. There is a big difference between moving quickly and learning on the fly and acting willy-nilly without regard to consequences.

Winston Churchill's statement, "Perfection is the enemy of progress" is timeless. An easy example for me is in the design aspects of the products we manufacture. Conceiving of and manufacturing cool items that excite me is one of the fun parts of what I do. However, it's too easy to get lost in the details of colors, form factor, interface, and packaging to your satisfaction. The reality is that rent is due every month and the clock is ticking. We would have a blast belaboring all the fun points of a new item, but to what end? You learn to indulge yourself with the essential creative details that you enjoy to serve the project's need and to know when you need to make a decision and move on to the next task. Focus on progress, learning, and growing from the experience rather than dwelling on perfection, and you're more likely to get the results you want. Remember, the learning is in the doing—don't miss out on making progress by waiting for perfection.

WANT CHANGE. Evolution is change. Just as plants flourish under stress, you grow when circumstances change and new information is revealed as you progress. When you are making things happen, the resulting change means that things are moving along. If you are not changing, you are not evolving. Sometimes changes are things we didn't initiate, like losing a job or having a competitor copy a product. In either situation—change through progress or unexpected change—what matters most is your perception of it and if and how you can use it to your benefit. I've already urged you to make friends with failure, and we also want to be buddies with change. It's inevitable. In a course on Failing Faster that I've taught at the d.school, we reframed change as a tool for finding a fresh perspective, something we imposed on ourselves with ease and regularity.

Change doesn't have to be a huge, sweeping, dramatic event, like moving into a new office space or changing your career. To keep change in the front of your mind, do something as small as driving a different route to work or ordering something different at your regular dinner spot.

CHANGE CAN BE
A HARBINGER
OF POSSIBILITIES.

You should not only want and welcome change, but also make change a regular part of your practice and being.

BALANCE IN MOTION. Balance may sound stationary and fixed, but it is not a finite or stagnant position. Balance is a fluid, living, moving thing. It's the active maintenance of opposing tensions. Surfing an ocean wave is a perfect visual to illustrate this concept. When riding a wave, the surfer is continuously adjusting their posture, weight placement, arm gesture, and sightline—all to stay upright on their board, balanced atop a moving body of water that is pushing back against the surfboard (Newton's third law of motion in action!). In play are multiple forces: the flow of water, gravity, resistance, physics—many of the things we've covered in previous sections. When riding the wave of bringing ideas to life, balance is having the multiple yin and yang aspects of your work in harmony, with both forces serving your needs and their tensions giving you a customized dimension of strength. Balance in one second will shift in the next. So drop the quest to "find" balance; it's not a thing or place to discover. It's a fluid condition that you need to get into, and it takes intentional emotional and intellectual awareness to engage in balance over a lifetime.

THINKING. Failure and change are absolutely unavoidable and not unwanted (yes, that is a double negative). Many successes come after a string of failures. Without enduring failure, without going through changes, you will not get to success. A good, honest failure just means you are pushing the limits. Feel like you haven't had success in a while? It may just be that you haven't been failing enough to do great work.

EMBRACE CHANGE AND APPRECIATE FAILURE,
THEY WILL LET YOU KNOW WHAT YOU NEED TO DO TO FIND YOUR WAY.

DOING: CELEBRATE SUCKING. Everything has to start somewhere. Nobody and nothing arrives fully formed. It often takes errors and missteps to lock in on the right path or pursuit. It takes years of sucking before achieving mastery of practically anything. One of the best activities run by improv experts in my Creative Gym course is all about sucking. We put pairs of students in an escalating low-stakes/high-failure situation repeatedly and get them to cheer with their partner whenever they make a mistake. Within about 5 minutes of doing this activity, they trade the typical awkward guilt/pause of messing up for a breezy lighthearted cheer followed by a fluid continuation of the activity. This classic improv activity called Clap, Snap, Stomp will help condition you to wear your errors lightly.

1 **Find another person to do this activity with and stand in front of each other. For each round, count out loud per the directions that follow, alternating turns. If and when one of you flubs up, both partners must simultaneously throw both arms up and say "Hooray!" with great enthusiasm. Do each round two or three times.**

2 **Round One: You and your partner count to 3, alternating turns saying the next number in sequence: "1," "2," "3," "1," . . . Go as fast as you can!**

3 **Round Two: Same as Round One but replace your 1s with claps!**

Round Three: Same as Round Two but replace your 2s with snaps! 4

5 **Round Four: Same as Round Three but replace your 3s with stomps!**

Review what just happened. How did that go? Did you and your partner end up cheering a lot? What did you notice about your partner's behavior in the beginning of the activity when you messed up? How did the dynamic change as the activity progressed? 6

Remember that errors are sometimes welcome indications that an adjustment is needed. It's like that errant crumb on your mouth that you may be unaware of—you want someone to tell you it's there so you can wipe it off. The sooner you know, the quicker you can handle it. Learning to shake off errors with a smile and keep going will take you a long way.

POSSIBILITIES ARE INFINITE. THEIR POTENTIAL MAKES YOU GIDDY WITH EXCITEMENT. THE WORK ZIGZAGS YOU UP, DOWN, AND SIDEWAYS. AND THEN RIGHT BEFORE YOU FINISH A POSSIBILITY, THE NEXT ONE HAS ALREADY SWEPT YOU ONWARD!

THERE REALLY IS NO FINISH
WHEN IT COMES TO POSSIBILITIES.

Finishing a possibility is like finding balance, as we described earlier: it's not a destination, but a moment in time. There will come a moment when everything you've done in service of making something happen will feel realized *for you*. It's a continual process, the dance between you and all your potentials and possibilities. You learn something new each time you finish. Bring that wisdom with you, and apply it to the next possibility.

Here are some small nuances that may help you be more aware of when and how you are standing in the spot of your momentary completion. Like a good outfit, you want to feel wonderful wearing it, even if it's just for the minute you catch your reflection in the window as you're passing by.

TO FINISH, FIND THE SWEET SPOT

In microeconomics, there is a concept called the point of diminishing returns, when adding more production or repeating a task has less and less output or impact. I use this concept a lot when negotiating curfews with my son. We try to teach him that nothing good happens after midnight—that there is a point during an evening (usually around midnight) when the fun at the party is maximized, and the longer you stay, the more the level of fun diminishes—or even takes a turn for the worse. This is definitely true when studying for finals in college and for entrepreneurial efforts where you really need to keep things moving. This is also true for your possibilities. The incremental value from additional effort may or may not be worth the time or the energy.

Knowing how to identify the point of diminishing returns is critical. Once you can recognize this, then you can decide what to do next. Sometimes you need to grind it into the ground; other times you need to move on to the next possibility. Whichever you choose to do is up to you, your needs, and the circumstances.
GO: GRIND ON OR MOVE ON.

TO FINISH, **BE YOUR OWN JUDGE**

It's up to you to give yourself confidence. You get confidence through doing, so go on and do! Complete a task, and your confidence will increase. How you measure an outcome is intensely personal because the value of an experience or outcome depends on its context *to you*. Your purpose, vision, and goal are part of your possibilities, the primary lens through which worth should be measured.

Quit trying to impress others around you. Do not allow constructs like awards, third-party recognition, and social media likes to determine your progress, accomplishment, or worth. These various artificial methods of recognition are fabricated marketing tools. For most people, it's human nature to desire to be liked, appreciated, and recognized. But why subject your self-worth to an external societal construct? It's so limiting! Only you know the true meaning of your possibility, and only you can plot its journey to completion. When you do not leave the barometer of your achievement in the hands of others, you can better assess where you are in your possibilities journey.

GO: ONLY YOU CAN DETERMINE THE VALUE OF WHAT YOU ACHIEVE AND DO.

TO FINISH, REALIZE IT'S NOT ABOUT THE THING

In the early days of the d.school, the founders created a famous introductory design project called The Wallet Project. It is a very straightforward activity in which the participant cycles through the design thinking methodology. It starts with the challenge of building a better wallet for another person. At the end of the experience, participants realize that they are actually solving to improve not the wallet itself, but the *ways the wallet serves its owner.* "Wallet" is not about a way to hold your license, cards, and money; it's a way for Jennifer to feel connected to her children while she is away at work or for Bob to feel financially secure. It's really about the process for solving for the wallet owner's needs, not about the wallet itself. It's interesting to see a pile of physical prototypes of "better wallets" resulting from the activity, but those wallets are not the finish. The finish is the identification of what Jennifer needs from her wallet and solving for that. The real ending is not what you make but

what you take with you—the doing and learning and practice you use to make your possibilities happen.
GO: LEAN INTO THE PROCESS, NOT THE THING.

TO FINISH, **PLEASE PAUSE**

Taking a moment does not have to be a month-long sabbatical in Greece. A 15-minute walk outside, a nice long hot shower, a lingering gaze out your window will all do the trick. The point is that we all need to take a break. And during this time, give thanks for where you currently are and your progress. Reflect on how things are going and appreciate yourself and the moment. This rest is an organic way for your mind to press pause, which not only provides a moment of quiet and focus but also allows your brain to synthesize something new to embark on.
GO: TAKE A BREATHER AND APPRECIATE HOW FAR YOU HAVE COME.

TO FINISH, **KEEP GOING**

I recently attended a family friend's memorial service. This young man was so vibrant, curious, loving, and giving in his abbreviated years. And in an unexpected moment, he was no longer with us. It reminded me that we are born and then we die. What stands in between those two life markers are all our possibilities. It's a privilege to be able to create something of value to help, serve, equalize, provide, surprise, inspire, comfort, enable, amplify, aid, and delight people with our efforts. It's pretty amazing to imagine what we can do with our time. So I urge you to go out and engage your possibilities!

SEE

Be curious and marvel at each and every glorious detail. Formulate a clear vision for your possibility until you can smell it.

START

You have the capacity to make stuff happen for yourself and others. Put away your brain, put on your heart, roll up your sleeves, and begin.

DO

Give the entirety of yourself fully to every moment, follow your wonder, and feast on the abundance of this universe that surrounds you.

FINISH

Soak up the process, and remember to reflect on what you've accomplished without regard to anyone's judgment but your own.

My ambition with this book is to fortify and transform you and your ideas in service of a better *everything*. Though the work in this book focuses on you, making possibilities happen is a recipe for creating change in the world and an outlook to help us all grow together. Yes, you can! Possibility is here for your making.

GO: MAKE SOMETHING HAPPEN.

ACKNOWLEDGMENTS

This work was once just a possibility seeded long ago. Your being here was also seeded long ago.

Just how long ago? During a recent visit to my childhood home in southern California, I came across my journals from middle school through college. While flipping through my cringey analog adolescent and young adult scribbles of decades past, my eye caught some glimmering fragments, some innocuous entries, that point to possibility and this book:

2/18/86 *Things can happen if you make them happen.*

9/1/90 *Someday is today—it's everyday.*

11/14/91 *"Where there is no vision, people perish."* *—Proverbs 29:18*

8/19/93 *You are everything you imagine. Live your vision. Just imagine and then be it.*

Even thirty years later, the handwritten thoughts still mean what they say. This made me reflect further on how this book actually came to be, and all the countless events, people, and encounters that led to its existence. So here are the salient events that led to *Make Possibilities Happen*:

▷ The fateful *Ambidextrous* zine field trip to *ReadyMade* magazine's HQ in Berkeley, California, taken by Charlotte Burgess-Auburn and Dr. Wendy Ju;

▷ d.school co-founder George Kembal's invitation;

▷ Hatching the Creative Gym course at Stanford's d.school in 2009 with Charlotte, Scott Doorley, and Dr. Julian Gorodsky (who knew at the time that our course would spawn so much goodness?);

▷ Dr. Daniel Hong's very simple question, "Is my brain different?";

▷ The years-long research project on creative capacity building led by Stanford Professor Dr. Allan Reiss's matching curiosity, the support of his Center for Interdisciplinary Brain Sciences Research, Assistant Professor Dr. Manish Saggar's work ethic, and the Hasso Plattner Institute–Stanford Design Thinking Research Program's generosity;

▷ Sarah Stein-Greenberg's initiative to green light *Make Space*;

▷ The evolution of activities teaching with Seamus Yu Harte;

▷ The unrelenting Stanford d.familia over the years who enable the meaning of possibilities in real life for the students and teaching teams daily;

▷ The willing and eager participation of students at Stanford that have graced the d.school studios;

▷ And the twelve years long—and still counting—gift of curious collaborations with Charlotte and Scott, on things both large and small (including this book!). It's all been amazing.

I have so much gratitude for everyone and every event above, including the following people for bringing this vision to life with such great care: The visually electric book design by the ever-talented creative director and designer Celia Leung (a decade-plus long collaborator too!) stands tall alongside the insightful guidance of project editor Jennifer Brown, and the wonderful folks at Ten Speed Press, including Kim Keller and the rest of the editorial, design, and production teams.

And where would I be physically and figuratively without my fierce, original-environmentalist parents for seeding my entrepreneurial spirit and relentless drive to create; my knower-of-all-things brother for having my back and the back of my words since I can remember; and my family for being my lifeline and purpose.

Since everything we create is part or parcel of something that came before us (see chapter 4), I'd like to point out some people and things that I regularly return to when a little kick in the butt is in order: *The Art of Looking Sideways* by Alan Fletcher, *As a Man Thinketh* by James Allen, *Ways of Seeing* by John Berger, *Printed Matter/ Drukwerk* by Karel Martens, *Impro* by Keith Johnstone, *The Wing on a Flea* by Ed Emberley, *The Last Whole Earth Catalog*, Marcel Duchamp, Buckminster Fuller, e.e. cummings, "Dig Down" by Muse, and nature in any form or time of day.

Much gratitude to you, the reader, for engaging with these words and for activating them in your life in service of a better tomorrow because anything *is* possible.

INDEX

Ten Speed Press and the Ten Speed Press colophon are registered trademarks
of Penguin Random House LLC.

Typefaces: Hope Meng's d.sign, Dinamo's Whyte and Whyte Inktrap,
and TypeType's Trailers

Library of Congress Cataloging-in-Publication Data
Names: Hawthorne, Grace H., author.
Title: Make Possibilities Happen : how to transform ideas into reality /
Grace Hawthorne.
Description: California : Ten Speed Press, [2023] |
Includes bibliographical references. | Summary: "A guide to imagining
the undiscovered and transforming your ideas into reality,
from Stanford University's d.school"— Provided by publisher.
Identifiers: LCCN 2022013209 (print) | LCCN 2022013210 (ebook) |
ISBN 9781984858122 (trade paperback) | ISBN 9781984858139 (ebook)
Subjects: LCSH: Creative ability. | Goal (Psychology) | Achievement motivation.
Classification: LCC BF408 .H388 2023 (print) | LCC BF408 (ebook) |
DDC 153.3/5—dc23/eng/20220914

LC record available at https://lccn.loc.gov/2022013209
LC ebook record available at https://lccn.loc.gov/2022013210

Trade Paperback ISBN: 978-1-9848-5812-2
eBook ISBN: 978-1-9848-5813-9

Printed in China

Acquiring editor: Hannah Rahill | Project editor: Kim Keller
Production editor: Sohayla Farman
Designer: Celia Leung | Art director: Emma Campion
Production designers: Annie Marino, Mari Gill, and Faith Hague
Production and prepress color manager: Jane Chinn
Copyeditor: Kristi Hein | Proofreader: Lisa Brousseau | Indexer: Ken DellaPenta
Publicist: Natalie Yera | Marketer: Chloe Aryeh
d.school creative team: Jenn Brown, Charlotte Burgess-Auburn, Scott Doorley